Bible Verse Fun with Kids

BIBLE VERSE FUN

with Kids

200+
Ideas & Activities
That Help Children
Learn & Live Scripture

CINDY DINGWALL

Abingdon Press
Nashville

BIBLE VERSE FUN WITH KIDS:

200+ IDEAS & ACTIVITIES THAT HELP CHILDREN LEARN & LIVE SCRIPTURE

Copyright © 2004 by Cindy Dingwall

This book is printed on acid-free paper.

ISBN 0-687-04514-2

Library of Congress Cataloging-in-Publication Data

Dingwall, Cindy.
  Bible verse fun with kids : 200 + ideas & activities that help children learn & live Scripture / Cindy Dingwall.
    p. cm.
  Summary: Bible verses, related writings, puzzles, games, and crafts help children learn Bible stories, and service projects help them to live what they learn.
  Includes bibliographical references and index.
  ISBN 0-687-04514-2 (pbk. : alk. paper)
  1. Bible—Study and teaching (Elementary)—Activity programs. 2. Christian education of children. [1. Bible—Study and teaching.
2. Christian life.] I. Title.

BS600.3.D56 2004
268'.432—dc22

2003021795

To my friend and former teacher, Kerry Tomb,
who inspired me to always do my best

CONTENTS

ACKNOWLEDGMENTS

Many thanks to

The Reverend Hannah Will, pastor of Church of the Incarnation, for her prayers and assistance in answering my many questions.

The staff of the Prospect Heights Public Library in Prospect Heights, Illinois, who encourage all of my creative ideas. Special thanks to the Youth Services Staff: Sue Seggeling, Head of the Youth Services Department, Alice Johnson, Kathy Stiles, Karolyn Nance, and Glen Poch.

All of my friends who help keep my faith strong through their continued prayers and encouragement.

My West Highland white terrier, Tara, who snuggles by my feet as I create and write.

— *Cindy Dingwall*

INTRODUCTION

Bible Verse Fun with Kids overflows with enjoyable activities designed to help kids in grades 1 through 5 learn and remember twenty-five Bible verses. Stories, music, games, crafts, puzzles, and more will make learning Scripture fun and easy. As children explore these Bible verses, they will be able to explain the meaning of the verse in their own words. Children will discover the verse as they play games, listen to stories, and work on projects together, and they will find encouragement to remember each Bible verse by using the various puzzles and activities that are included.

In addition, each chapter includes suggested books that enhance the chapter lesson. The material in Bible Verse Fun with Kids is arranged in biblical order; however, feel free to use the verses in any order you choose. Throughout the book, you will find worship tie-ins that can be used as children's messages shared during congregational worship. Invite your pastor, the Christian education director, or another member of your church to share these with the children. Worship tie-ins can also be used as activities the children can do to lead worship (for example, write and offer a prayer or litany or sing a song). You might consider focusing the entire congregation—adults, youth, and children to learn and remember the selected verse each week.

While a suggested Bible story is included with most chapters, some chapters encourage you to select your own favorite Bible story to share with the children. Each lesson includes a project that encourages children to do a service that helps others. Adapt activities as needed to accommodate children with disabilities in your group. A puzzle accompanies each Bible verse. Children can do these during class or take them home to complete.

In the appendix, you will find Bible verse games and Bible verse activities. Children will discover how many Bible verses they can remember in three entertaining games. This section provides activities for the various verses included in this book.

The ideas and activities in Bible Verse Fun with Kids are designed to make learning Scripture enjoyable. Now go forth and let the word of God dwell in you richly as you go about helping kids remember God's words of love and encouragement.

BEFORE YOU BEGIN

1. Begin planning early. Plan your lesson several weeks in advance.
2. Read through each chapter carefully before sharing the lesson and activities. Make sure you have all of the materials needed for the lesson. Visit your public or school library if you need to check out books and look for additional materials (books, videos, recordings) that will enhance the lesson. Check bookstores for new materials that may help illustrate your lessons.
3. Have the room set up and ready to go before the children arrive. Be sure your art materials are set up and ready to use. Make a sample of the art project prior to the program.
4. Although these lessons have been designed so that one activity flows naturally into another, feel free to adapt them to meet the different needs of the children you serve.
5. Check to see if children have any food allergies before offering food snacks. Be willing to substitute foods, or ask parents and guardians to bring suitable foods for the children to eat.
6. Make all of your programs fragrance-free. Many children and adults suffer from chemical sensitivities that make them highly allergic to perfumes, scented soaps, lotions, shaving products, and hair products. Supply fragrance-free tissues.
7. Enlist the assistance of your youth group and adult volunteers to help with the programs. Meet with them prior to the program so they know how to best assist you and the children.
8. Begin promptly. Be fair to those who arrive on time. Avoid restarting or recapping for latecomers, as this disrupts the flow of the program.
9. Use a variety of storytelling techniques. The use of flannel boards, story cards, props, puppets, and creative dramatics brings stories alive.
10. Supply enrichment activities that highlight each lesson. Have these available for those who finish a project and need to occupy themselves while waiting for the others to finish. Puzzles, games, books, recordings that highlight each lesson can be used for this purpose.

WALKIN' WITH THE LORD

I will walk among you and be your God, and you will be my people.

—Leviticus 26:12 NIV

PROGRAM

GAME: WALKIN' WITH GOD (See page 10.)

DISCUSSION

Talk about the meaning of the Bible verse. What does God mean by "I will walk among you"? What does it mean to be people of God?

BIBLE STORY

Choose a favorite Bible story that involves people walking. Explain that in Bible times people traveled by walking. Talk about how Jesus walked during his ministry.

SONG: "GOIN' FOR A WALK WITH JESUS" RAP

(Let children take turns playing the role of Jesus. Jesus leads the others as they walk around the room chanting this rap. Each child chooses the actions for each verse.)

Refrain:

We're goin' for a walk, goin' for a walk, goin' for a walk
with Jesus. (stamp, stamp)
We're goin' for a walk, goin' for a walk, goin' for a walk
with Jesus! (stamp, stamp)

Verse:

Gonna kneel down and pray, gonna kneel down and pray,

gonna kneel down and pray for _____. (Let Jesus decide what to pray for, or let children offer one-word prayer responses.)

Refrain:

(Let Jesus think of other things to do. Chant the refrain between each verse.)

 **ART: GOD ALWAYS WALKS WITH ME**

(See page 10.)

 ACTIVITY: WENT FOR A WALK

(See pages 12-13.)

 PROJECT: "WALKIN' FOR THE LORD" WALKATHON (See page 11.)

 **BULLETIN BOARD: I WILL WALK AMONG YOU** (See page 12.)

WORSHIP TIE-IN: A FIELD TRIP

Gather the children at the altar and tell them you are going on a walking field trip around the sanctuary. Remind them that Jesus and his followers often walked about as they learned things. Tell the children about a variety of things in the sanctuary, for example, stained glass windows, organ, baptismal font, altar, banners, choir loft, and so on.

SOMETHING SPECIAL

Say It!
by Charlotte Zolotow
A little girl and her mother go for a wonderful autumn walk.

Footprints in the Sand
by Mary Stevenson

Chapter 1

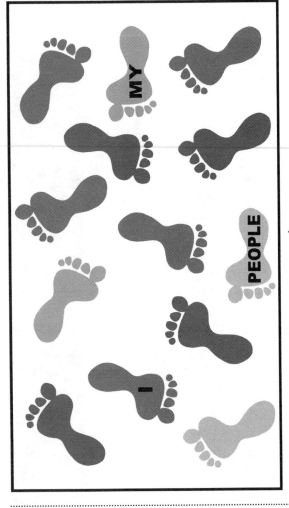

GAME: WALKIN' WITH GOD

Materials

a man's large feet, clear contact paper, colored construction paper, pencil, lively cassette or CD and cassette or CD player, scissors, black marker, white paper, masking tape

Preparation

1. Trace the man's feet onto white paper. Cut the feet out.
2. Trace the feet pattern onto colored construction paper. Make 3 to 5 feet in each color.
3. Use the black marker to print one word of the Bible verse Leviticus 26:12 on the bottom of a foot. One foot will have *Leviticus* printed on it, one foot will have *26:* printed on it, and another foot will have *12* printed on it. When finished, 16 feet will have words printed on them. Use as many different shades of paper as possible for the feet that have writing. You should have many feet without words as well.
4. Cover all of the feet with clear contact paper.
5. Tape the feet to the floor. The feet with the words should be taped with the words facing the floor.

Directions

1. Have each child stand on one paper foot.
2. As the music plays, have the children walk around the room.
3. When the music stops, have the children find a foot to stand on. Call out a color, for example, red. Anyone standing on a red foot will pick it up and look for a word. Have the children who find words bring them to you. Feet without words go back on the floor.
4. Play again until all the 16 feet with the verse printed on them are found. Let the kids help figure out the correct order of the words. Tape the feet to the floor so the verse is displayed in the correct order, or tape the feet to the floor of a long hallway in your church. That way everyone can enjoy walking down the "foot" path and reading the Bible verse.

GAME: WALKIN' WITH GOD ⇧

ART: GOD ALWAYS WALKS WITH ME

Materials

white paper, scissors, 1 photo of each child, glue, natural-colored sand, yarn, clear book tape, clear contact paper, 1 copy of the Bible verse Leviticus 26:12 for each child, beige construction paper, 1 sheet of powder blue cardboard per child (8-by-10-inches or 9-by-11-inches), a man's large foot

Preparation

1. Trace a man's large foot onto a piece of white paper. Type a copy of the verse that will fit inside the foot shape.
2. Photocopy the foot with verse onto beige paper. Trim the edges around the foot. Cover each foot with clear contact paper, and trim off excess.
3. Use book tape to tape a yarn loop on the back of each piece of blue cardboard.

Directions

1. Let the children each glue one foot to right side of the blue cardboard.
2. Let kids smear glue all around the footprint. Next, sprinkle sand onto the glue. Shake off excess sand.
3. Have each child glue his or her photograph to the left of the foot on the cardboard. Let dry.

I will walk
among you and
be your God,
and
you
will
be my
people.
– Leviticus
26:12 NIV

PROJECT: "WALKIN' FOR THE LORD" WALKATHON

Preparation

1. Choose a date and place for your intergenerational walkathon. Map out a safe route between 1 to 5 miles in length.
2. Ask church members, friends, neighbors, and coworkers to pledge an amount per mile walked.

3. Decide which agency will benefit from your profits (for example, Habitat for Humanity, a shelter, or food pantry).
4. Design eye-catching posters to advertise your walk.
5. Place mileage markers along the route at every half mile point. This helps people stay on the route and track their distance. Have two church members stationed at each marker. Consider supplying water, lemonade, cookies, and cheese and crackers for walkers.

Directions

1. On the day of the walk, have everyone meet at the starting point. Say a group prayer asking for safety for the walkers, giving thanks to the sponsors, and giving thanks to the Lord for bestowing the ability to walk to help others.
2. Begin walking. Let people walk as far as they want. If they choose to double back, count that distance as part of their mileage.

HINTS

+ As a safety precaution, people should walk in groups of two or more

+ Have one person in each group carry a working cell phone to call for help if needed

+ Provide a map of the walking course to each participant

+ Have 1-2 adults with each small group of children

+ Have a vehicle at each mile to transport people in need of help to the finish or back to the starting point

BULLETIN BOARD: I WILL WALK AMONG YOU

Materials

candid photos of children (individual or group shots), a man's large feet, blue tempera paint, paintbrush, white heavy duty paper large enough to cover your bulletin board, glue, permanent black marker

Preparation

1. Lay the paper on a hard floor.
2. Paint the man's feet blue and have him walk across the white paper.
3. After the footprints are dry, use a permanent black marker to print the words to the verse Leviticus 26:12 on each footprint.

Directions

Let the children glue the photos on the white paper. Leave a white border between the footprints and photos so it looks like a path going through the pictures. Take care not to cover the footprints.

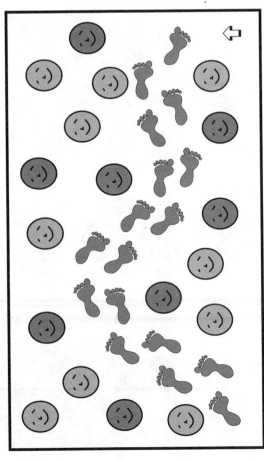

ACTIVITY: WENT FOR A WALK

Make this story into a flannel board. You will need the following patterns: blue sky, white cloud, sun, rainbow, grass, tree, bird, deer, butterfly, puppy, lake, and flowers. Use precut images or create your own. To create the images: (1) use a flannel board pattern book, like those listed in the bibliography, (2) lay interfacing over each pattern and trace, and (3) color the fabric using crayons. Share this story with the children. Divide the children into two groups. The first group can ask the question, while the second group gives the answer. Invite the children to share the story during worship.

Went for a walk, and what did I see?

I saw my parents waving good-bye to me! (children wave good-bye)

Went for a walk, and what did I see?

I saw the blue sky way above me!

Went for a walk, and what did I see?

I saw the sun shining way above me!

Went for a walk, and what did I see?

I saw a white cloud floating over me!

Went for a walk, and what did I see?

I saw a rainbow arching over me!

Went for a walk, and what did I see?

PUZZLE: LET'S TAKE A WALK

Start at the shaded box. If you color the correct spaces, you will find the path that has the Bible verse. Be careful—you don't want to go down the wrong path!

I	WALK	TWENTY	SIX	TWELVE	BE
WILL	LEVITICUS	WALK	I	GOD	PEOPLE
PEOPLE	GOD	YOU	WALK	AMONG	WALK
MY	WILL	**I** (shaded)	WILL	BE	YOU
BE	WALK	WALK	AMONG	AND	GOD
SHALL	TWENTY	LEVITICUS	YOUR	BE	TWELVE
YOU	SIX	GOD	YOU	WALK	AMONG
TWELVE	AND	BE	I	WILL	YOU

I saw the grass, right under me!

Went for a walk, and what did I see?

I saw a tree standing by me!

Went for a walk, and what did I see?

I saw lots of flowers all around me!

Went for a walk, and what did I see?

I saw a bird flying over me!

Went for a walk, and what did I see?

I saw a butterfly flying past me!

Went for a walk, and what did I see?

I saw a deer looking at me!

Went for a walk, and what did I see?

I saw a lake right in front of me!

Went for a walk and what did I see?

I saw my puppy following me!

Went for a walk, and what did I see?

I saw my friends waiting for me! (children wave to friends)

Went for a walk, and what did I see?

I saw God's love all around me!

Chapter 2

ROCKIN' WITH THE LORD

He is the Rock, his works are perfect, and all his ways are just.
—Deuteronomy 32:4 NIV

PROGRAM

GAME: STEPPING STONES (See page 15.)

DISCUSSION

Talk about God being our solid rock. Ask the kids to share their thoughts on this.

BIBLE STORY: THE TEN COMMANDMENTS

(Exodus 20:1-17)

Tell this story to the children. Explain that Moses was led to the top of Mount Sinai where God gave him the Ten Commandments. Explain that the Ten Commandments must be our foundation for living a good, solid Christian life.

ACTIVITY: ROCK HUNT (See page 16.)

SONG: "OH, THE LORD IS MY ROCK" RAP

Find upbeat instrumental music. Ask the kids to recite the following lines while the music plays. An alternative is to let them use drums and other rhythm instruments that make interesting sounds while reciting the rap.

Oh, the Lord . . . he is my rock . . . my rock and salvation.
I build my love on the rock of God.
God gives me strength. God helps me all the time.
God's love for me is as solid as this rock! And I love him too . . . oh yes I do!

ART: ROCK DOORSTOP (See page 16.)

ACTIVITY: COMPUTER ROCKS

Let the children search for other verses about rocks using an electronic concordance. Have them copy the verses onto rock shaped pieces of gray and brown construction paper with a black marker. These will be used to create the bulletin board on pages 16-17.

BULLETIN BOARD: ROCKIN' WITH JESUS! (See pages 16-17.)

PROJECT: ROCK DOORSTOPS

Let the children make rock doorstops that they will sell to members of the congregation. The money can be donated to an agency that provides disaster relief to children whose homes have been destroyed by natural disasters. See Art on page 16 for instructions.

WORSHIP TIE-IN: SOLID AS A ROCK

You'll need a hammer, a hard-boiled egg, a cookie sheet, and a large rock for this worship tie-in. Test the rock beforehand to make sure it can withstand a hammer strike. Invite the kids to come to the altar. Talk about having a strong faith in God. Put the egg on the cookie sheet. Smash it with the hammer. Explain that when we don't have faith in God, we will break just like the egg did. We won't have the strength to withstand the challenges life has to offer. Hit the rock with the hammer. Explain that if we have a strong faith in God, we will have the strength to face life's challenges.

SOMETHING SPECIAL

It Could Still Be a Rock by Allan Fowler
God created rocks in all sizes, shapes, and forms. Each rock has a special place in God's world.

The Rock by Peter Parnell
The rock provided a home, shelter, food, and a place to sit for all of God's creatures.

GAME: STEPPING STONES

Materials

gray paper, scissors, masking tape, large sheet of blue paper (about 6 feet by 18 feet), black permanent marker, laminating film and machine or clear contact paper, 1 large box, upbeat Christian music cassette or CD and cassette or CD player

Preparation

1. Cut 30 to 50 large rocks from the gray paper.
2. Print one word of the verse Deuteronomy 32:4 on a different rock. Fourteen rocks will have words printed on them. Print *Deuteronomy* on one rock, *32:* on another rock, and *4* on another. Some of the rocks will be without words. Cover the rocks with contact paper or laminate them.
3. Cut the blue paper so it looks like a long, wide river. Laminate it or cover it with contact paper.
4. Secure the river to the floor with masking tape. Next, tape rocks words-down so that they appear to go across the river.

Directions

1. As the music plays, each child takes a turn walking on the rocks to cross the river. Stop the music and have the child pick up the rock he or she is standing on.

2. If the selected rock has a word on it, lay it along the riverbank. If the rock does not have a word, the children return it to the floor. Those landing on rocks without words keep playing until they land on a rock that reveals a word.
3. After all of the rocks with words and numbers have been uncovered, let the children see if they can put the verse in the correct order.

GAME: STEPPING STONES ⇨

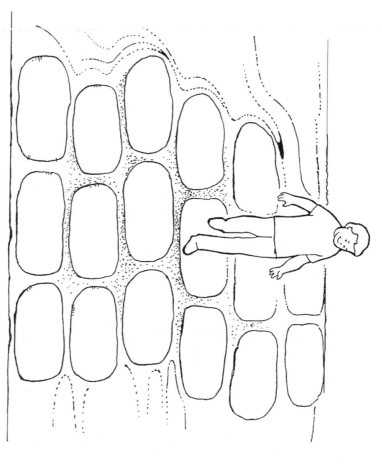

ACTIVITY: ROCK HUNT

Materials
1 or more child-sized swimming pools, sand, gravel, dirt, grass, several different kinds of rocks, shovels, sifters

Preparation
1. Fill the pool or pools with sand, gravel, dirt, and grass.
2. Hide the rocks in the layers of materials you have in the pools.

Directions
1. Explain how geologists dig for rocks beneath the surface of the earth.
2. Divide the kids into teams. Let each team use the shovels, sifters, and other tools to search for rocks hidden beneath the surface of the earth.
3. Research the different types of rocks on hand. Talk about how rocks make up part of the earth. Why did God make rocks a part of the earth's structure? Talk about the uses we have for rocks. Show children the difference between gravel, stones, rocks, and boulders. Discuss God's love and strength symbolized in the strength of a rock.

ART: ROCK DOORSTOP

Materials
1 large heavy rock per child, paints, decoupage solution, one copy of the Bible verse Deuteronomy 32:4 per child, 1 paint-brush per child, laminating film and machine or clear contact paper

Preparation
Cover the Bible verses with laminating film or clear contact paper.

Directions
1. Let each child paint his or her rock, if they wish.
2. Give each child a Bible verse. Let them decoupage the verse to the rock. Let dry.
3. Kids can take these home to use as doorstops and make several to sell for the Project (page 14).

BULLETIN BOARD: ROCKIN' WITH JESUS!

Materials
gray and brown construction paper rocks from the "Computer Rocks" activity (see page 14), purple, blue, green, yellow, and brown construction paper, clear contact paper, black markers, letter stencils or dye cut machine, white cotton balls, scissors, picture of Jesus (create your own or use a premade one)

Preparation
1. Cover the bulletin board with blue construction paper. Use the green paper to make hills and leaves for the tree.

2. Use brown paper to make a tree trunk and branches. Make a sun from the yellow paper. Add the cotton clouds.
3. Print the Bible verse Deuteronomy 32:4 onto a white word cloud and attach it to the board.

Directions

Have the children add the rocks with the Bible verses to the scene. Add a picture of Jesus.

> He is the Rock, his works are perfect, and all his ways are just. Deuteronomy 32:4

rocks with scriptures on them

BULLETIN BOARD: ROCKIN' WITH JESUS! ⇨

PUZZLE: ROCKIN' WITH GOD

What kind of a rock climber are you? Start at the bottom, and make your way to the top. Use the right rocks and reveal the hidden Bible verse.

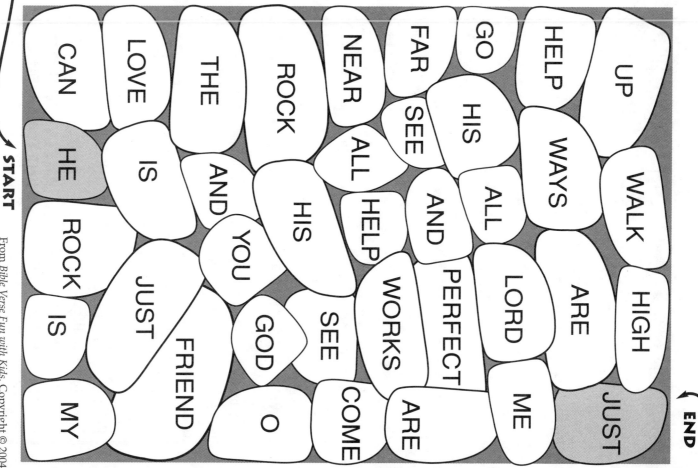

START

END

Chapter 3

IN GOD'S HAND

In his hand is the life of every living thing and the breath of every human being.

—Job 12:10

PROGRAM

GAME: HIDDEN HANDS (See page 19.)

BIBLE STORY: JESUS HEALS A SHRIVELED HAND (Matthew 12:9-13 and Mark 3:1-5)

Tell this story to the children. Talk about how Jesus used his hands to heal and help people.

SONG: "HE'S GOT THE WHOLE WORLD IN HIS HANDS"

Encourage the children to think of things and people in God's hands. Let the children sing this song for congregational worship.

SOMETHING SPECIAL

These Hands
by Hope Lynne Price
A little girl discovers all of the marvelous things she can do with her hands.

ART: "IN GOD'S HAND" WALL HANGING (See pages 19-20.)

SONG: "IN HIS HAND" *("If You're Happy")*

In his hand, in his hand, in his hand! *(clap, clap)*
Is the life of every living thing! *(clap, clap)*
In his hand, in his hand, in his hand,
Is the breath of every human being! *(clap, clap)*

Let the children create additional verses. (Is the breath of every bird, dog, kid, dad, and so on.)

PROJECT: HANDS THAT HELP

Help the children think of a service project they can do with their hands, for example: cleaning the yard, cooking a meal for homebound neighbor, or creating cards for hospitalized church members.

BULLETIN BOARD: HELPING HANDS (See page 20.)

WORSHIP TIE-IN: IN HIS HAND

Invite the children to sing this song during congregational worship. Prior to the service make several large posters that have a picture of a large hand holding one of the things the children will sing about, for example, animals and pets. As they sing about a creature, the child holding that poster can hold it up for all to see.

DISCUSSION

Talk about things we do with our hands. How can we use our hands to help others?

ACTIVITY: LOOK, NO HANDS! (See page 19.)

GAME: HIDDEN HANDS

Materials

colored construction paper, white paper, scissors, markers, laminating film and machine or clear contact paper, black marker

Preparation

1. Make a hand pattern from your own hand or a child's hand on white paper. Using the pattern, make 17 colorful construction paper hands. Print one word from the verse Job 12:10 on each hand.
2. Laminate the hands or cover them with clear contact paper.
3. Choose hiding places for the hands depending upon the children's ages and abilities.

Directions

1. Tell the children to hunt for the hidden hands. When a child finds a hand, have them return to the seating area.
2. Have the children arrange themselves in a circle with the verse reading in the correct order. Let each child read the word from his or her hand. Then have the entire group read the verse together.

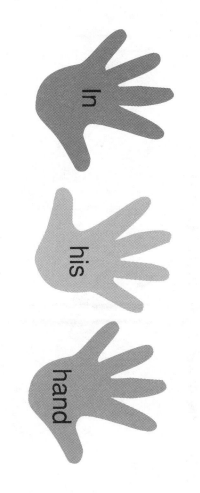

In

his

hand

ACTIVITY: LOOK, NO HANDS!

Let the children try to do things without using their hands, for example, play with balloons, write, and get dressed. Use yarn to gently tie the children's hands behind their backs. Talk about what it would be like to live without the use of our hands. Tell the children about Joni Eareckson Tada who is a quadriplegic. Explain that she uses her mouth to paint. Give the kids paintbrushes, paint, and paper. Let the children see if they can paint and write using only their mouths. See what other challenges you can create for the children to do without their hands.

ART: "IN GOD'S HAND" WALL HANGING

Materials

1 school or instant photo of each child, cardboard, decoupage glue, hole punch, one 12-inch strand of yarn per child, scissors, 1 large paintbrush per child, cut out magazine pictures of animals, plants, flowers, people, and other things God has created, waterproof marker

Preparation

1. Cut each child's photo into a circle.
2. Create a pattern of your own hand or a child's hand. Enlarge the pattern and cut a large hand for each child from cardboard.

3. Use waterproof marker to print the Bible verse Job 12:10 on the back of each hand.

Directions

1. Give each child a cardboard hand and a paintbrush.
2. Let kids select which magazine pictures they want to use to cover their hands.
3. Show the kids how to use the brushes and decoupage glue to attach the photos to the front of their hands. Make sure they leave the back empty of pictures, so the verse can be read.
4. When the hands are covered with pictures, give each child his or her photo and tell him or her to decoupage that to the center of the hand.
5. Let the hands dry completely. Then trim off the excess edges.
6. Punch a hole in the top of the hand. String the hands with yarn, so they can be hung.

BULLETIN BOARD: HELPING HANDS

Materials

white butcher paper for background, colored tempera paints, paintbrushes for each color, stapler, letter stencils or dye cut machine, scissors, colored thin-tipped felt markers (dark blue, purple, dark green, red), white and colored construction paper (yellow, orange, light blues, greens)

Preparation

Cut colored construction paper into 3-by-1/2-inch strips.

Directions

1. Use the stencils or dye cut machine to make the letters HELPING HANDS from the white construction paper. Cut the letters out and set them aside.
2. Lay the white paper on a large table.
3. Let the children decide what colors to paint their hands. Have the kids make handprints all over the white paper, covering most of the whiteness.
4. Give each child a slip of colored paper and a colored marker. Let them use the colored markers to write how they can use their hands to help others.
5. Staple the handprinted background to the bulletin board. Staple the title and the slips of paper to the bulletin board.

BULLETIN BOARD: HELPING HANDS ⇧

Cross out the X's. The left over letters spell out a message. Print the message on the lines below.

_____

_____

_____

_____

_____

IXNHIXXSXHANXD
ISXXXTXHXELIX
FXEXXXXOFXXXE
XVERYXXLIVXING
XXTXHXIXNXGXAX
XXXNDTHEBXREATXH
XXXXOFXXEVXERYXXXXH
XXUMXAXNXXXBXEXIXX
XXXXNXXXXXXXGXX

From *Bible Verse Fun with Kids*. Copyright © 2004 by Cindy Dingwall. Reprinted by permission.

Chapter 4

LET THE WORDS OF MY MOUTH

Let the words of my mouth and the meditation of my heart be acceptable to you, O LORD, my rock and my redeemer.

—Psalm 19:14

PROGRAM

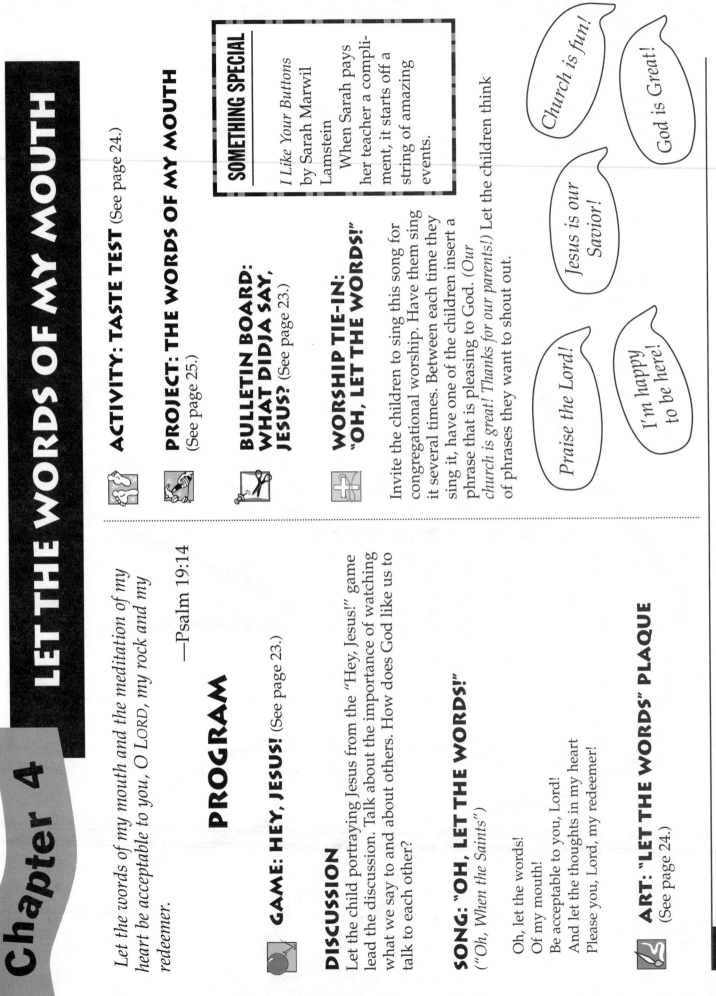

GAME: HEY, JESUS! (See page 23.)

DISCUSSION
Let the child portraying Jesus from the "Hey, Jesus!" game lead the discussion. Talk about the importance of watching what we say to and about others. How does God like us to talk to each other?

SONG: "OH, LET THE WORDS!"
(*"Oh, When the Saints"*)

Oh, let the words!
Of my mouth!
Be acceptable to you, Lord!
And let the thoughts in my heart
Please you, Lord, my redeemer!

ART: "LET THE WORDS" PLAQUE
(See page 24.)

ACTIVITY: TASTE TEST (See page 24.)

PROJECT: THE WORDS OF MY MOUTH
(See page 25.)

BULLETIN BOARD: WHAT DIDJA SAY, JESUS? (See page 23.)

WORSHIP TIE-IN: "OH, LET THE WORDS!"

Invite the children to sing this song for congregational worship. Have them sing it several times. Between each time they sing it, have one of the children insert a phrase that is pleasing to God. (*Our church is great! Thanks for our parents!*) Let the children think of phrases they want to shout out.

Church is fun!

Jesus is our Savior!

God is Great!

Praise the Lord!

I'm happy to be here!

GAME: HEY, JESUS!

Materials

24 beanbags, 24 slips of paper, colored felt markers, volunteer to portray Jesus, duct tape, basket

Preparation

1. Print one word of the verse Psalm 19:14 on each slip of paper. Use rolled duct tape to attach each word slip to a beanbag. Write the scripture reference on one bag.
2. Put the beanbags into the basket.

Directions

1. Have Jesus enter the room carrying the basket of beanbags.

Teach the children this rhyme in a rap style rhythm:

Hey, Jesus! What ya got to say? What ya got to say, to me today?

2. One at a time, have each child face Jesus and say the rhyme.

Jesus will respond with:

Hey, (child's name), this is what I say!
This is what I gotta say to you today!

Jesus will toss a beanbag to each child.

3. When each child has a beanbag, have the group place the verse in the correct order, then say it together.

BULLETIN BOARD: WHAT DIDJA SAY, JESUS?

Materials

1 Bible that has the words of Jesus in red per child or group, white construction paper, colored markers, large picture of Jesus

Preparation

Cut one word cloud from white construction paper for each child.

Directions

1. Kids can work individually or in groups of 2 to 4 people.
2. Give each child or group a Bible and have them turn to the Gospels. Let each child or group search a different section of a book or a section of a book.
3. Tell everyone to search for the words in red since these are the words that Jesus spoke. Each child or group should select a verse they like.
4. Use the markers to neatly print the verse on a word cloud.
5. Place the picture of Jesus on a blank wall or bulletin board and arrange the word clouds around him.
6. Discuss the verses.

You shall love your neighbor as yourself.
Mark 12:31

Blessed are the pure in heart, for they will see God.
Matthew 5:8

Do to others as you would have them do to you.
Matthew 7:12

Peace be with you.
John 20:19

ART: "LET THE WORDS" PLAQUE

Materials

1 instant or school photo of each child, one 5-by-7-inch wooden plaque per child, wood stain and brushes, 1 copy of the Bible verse Psalm 19:14 per child, decoupage solution, 1 paintbrush per child, 1 metal plaque hanger per child, clear contact paper, colored pencils, newspaper, waxed paper

Preparation

1. Attach plaque hangers to the backs of the plaques.
2. Stain the plaques, and allow them to dry completely.
3. Use the computer to type and print a copy of the Bible verse for each child. Choose an attractive, easy-to-read font.

Directions

1. Give each child a copy of the Bible verse. Let the children use the colored pencils to draw a colorful border around the outside edges of the verse.

Let the words of my mouth and the meditation of my heart be acceptable to you O Lord, my rock and my redeemer.
— Psalm 19:14

2. Cover both sides of each child's verse with contact paper.
3. Have the kids use the brushes to apply decoupage solution to their plaques. Center the verse on the plaque for the children. Apply decoupage solution over the verse too.
4. Give each child his or her photo, and have him or her decoupage it to the plaque.
5. These will take awhile to dry. Give each child a piece of newspaper with a sheet of waxed paper on top of it. Place the plaque on top of the waxed paper to carry home.

ACTIVITY: "TASTE TEST"

Materials

vinegar or lemon juice, plastic spoon for each child, Kisses™, 1 blindfold per child, 2 bowls

Preparation

1. Pour some vinegar or lemon juice into a bowl.
2. Place the chocolate candies in a bowl.

Directions

1. Have the kids sit in a circle. Blindfold the kids.
2. Tell the following story and follow the actions indicated.

It was a stormy day—way too wet and cold to play outside. It was thundering, and it was lightning, and the rain was pouring down hard. Jacob and Caitlynn had to play in the house all day long. And let me tell you, they didn't want to play inside. They were crabby and they fought all day long. And their dad was getting tired of hearing them squabble. Then Jacob accidentally knocked over Caitlynn's paint and it spilled on the picture she was painting.

"I'm sorry, Caitlynn," said Jacob.

"I hate you, you slimy, lumpy, smelly toad!" Caitlynn yelled at her brother Jacob. Jacob started to cry.

(Go around the room and use the spoons to put a small amount of vinegar or lemon juice into each child's mouth. They will not like the taste.)

Dad came into the room and scolded Caitlynn for what she had said.

"I don't care if I said something to make Jacob sad. He is a slimy, lumpy, smelly toad! And he spilled my paint all over my painting!"

"But Jacob said he was sorry. Caitlynn, God doesn't like it when we use our mouths and our words to hurt people," said Dad.

"God doesn't?" asked Caitlynn.

"No. Saying unkind things to others makes God very sad." Caitlynn looked at her little brother. She really didn't hate him. She was just mad at him because he had knocked over her paint.

"I'm sorry, Jacob. I guess it was an accident. You know what? Look at my painting now—it really looks cool after you spilled the paint on it. It's totally awesome!"

(Go around the room and using the spoons put a chocolate candy into each child's mouth.)

3. Discuss what happened in the story. Ask the kids if they have ever said mean, nasty, or hurtful things to others. Then ask if they have ever had something mean, nasty, or hurtful said to them. Ask: How does it feel when someone says something mean, nasty, or hurtful? Do you like it? Why not? What can we do and say when we are angry and upset with someone? How can we use our mouths and words to help and compliment others? How did it taste when I put the vinegar/lemon juice in your mouth? Not good! The vinegar's/lemon juice's bad taste is like the bad words. How did the chocolate taste? Good! The good taste reminds us of good words.

PROJECT: THE WORDS OF MY MOUTH

Materials

1 small notebook for each child

Directions

1. Challenge the children to say something nice to everyone they see and meet this week. Talk with them about kind, encouraging, and complimentary things they can say to others, such as, "That's a pretty blouse, Mrs. Nelson." "It was nice of you to help Katie with her math." "Sometimes it's hard to learn new stuff. I know you can learn to do it!"

2. Explain that people will wonder what they are doing and why. Discuss several ways they can explain why they are saying kind things. Share information about the project with parents, and ask for their help. Give each child a small notebook. Encourage them to write down the nice things they say to others and what the reaction of the recipient was. Have the children bring the notebooks to your next session and share their experiences.

3. Be prepared to discuss all of the things that happened as a result of their kind actions. Ask: Did people make fun of you for being kind? How did that make you feel? How did you feel when your compliments made others feel good? What other things happened when you complimented others?

PUZZLE: WATCH WHAT YOU SAY!

Cross out all of the faces that are not smiling. Can you figure out the message?

From *Bible Verse Fun with Kids*. Copyright © 2004 by Cindy Dingwall. Reprinted by permission.

Chapter 5

TEACH US TO PRAY

Hear my prayer, O God; give ear to the words of my mouth.

—Psalm 54:2

PROGRAM

GAME: PASS THE MESSAGE ON!

(See page 28.)

DISCUSSION

Discuss how the message in the previous game became garbled. When we don't pray and listen for God's instructions in our lives, we get the message wrong and we give wrong messages to others. Talk about why we pray. Ask: What do we pray for? Who do we pray for? How does praying help us? How does prayer help others? Why does Jesus want us to pray? Ask the children if we get everything we ask for in prayer. Discuss this with the children. Remind the children that God still loves us even if we do not get everything we ask for in prayer.

BIBLE STORIES

Discuss the different ways Jesus taught us to pray. Look at the Lord's Prayer (Matthew 6:9-13; Luke 11:1-4). Sometimes Jesus wants us to pray alone (Matthew 6:5). Sometimes Jesus wants us to pray with others (Matthew 18:20). Why do you think Jesus wants us to pray alone some of the time? Why does Jesus want us to pray together some of the time? Share the story of how Jesus prayed at the Mount of Olives (Luke 22:39-46). Tell the stories from John 17 where Jesus prays for himself, for his disciples, and for all believers. Talk about how Jesus prayed in the garden of Gethsemane (Matthew 26:36-42; Mark 14:32-37).

DISCUSSION

Talk about the different kinds of prayers: morning prayers, graces, bedtime prayers, prayers of thanksgiving, prayers for those in need, prayers before tests, and so on. Talk about prayer being a quiet time, a time when we can talk to God, a time when we can listen for God's voice.

Explain the Jewish custom of using prayer shawls. The Hebrew word for prayer shawl is *tallit*. A prayer shawl is a long, striped piece of material that has four corners. There are fringes at each corner. Each fringe has eight threads. The fringes remind us that we are called to follow the commandments of God. They remind us to resist temptation to sin. Some Jewish people put the prayer shawl around their shoulders before beginning their morning prayers. Today we are going to make prayer shawls.

(See page 28.)

SOMETHING SPECIAL

BOOK: *Emma & Mommy Talk to God* by Marianne Williamson

Emma's mother teaches her about the joy and importance of talking to God.

SONG: "Day by Day" by Stephen Schwartz (From the musical *Godspell*)

Help the children learn this song. Let them sing it for congregational worship. Invite the congregation to sing with the children.

ART: PRAYER SHAWLS

SONG: "HEAR MY PRAYER"
("Michael Row the Boat")

Hear my prayer, O God, hear my prayer!
Oh, give ear to the words of my mouth, O Lord!

PROJECT: PRAYER SERVICE (See page 29.)

BULLETIN BOARD: HEAR OUR PRAYER, O LORD (See page 29.)

WORSHIP TIE-IN: AND A LITTLE CHILD SHALL LEAD THEM
(See the Project on page 29.)

GAME: PASS THE MESSAGE ON!

Materials
white paper, colored markers

Preparation
Use the colored markers to print the Bible verse Psalm 54:2 on the paper. Keep this out of sight of the children until after they have played the game.

SOMETHING SPECIAL

The Always Prayer Shawl by Sheldon Oberman
A grandfather gives his prayer shawl to his young grandson who treasures it until it is time to hand it down to his own grandson.

Directions
1. Sit in a circle with the children.
2. Whisper the Bible verse Psalm 54:2 into the ear of the child on your right. That child will whisper the verse into the ear of the child on their right, and so on, all around the circle. Have the child on their right receive the message. Keep going until the last child receives the message. Have that child share the message with the others. The message has probably become garbled.
4. Show the paper with the Bible verse printed on it.
5. Talk about the verse as you heard it at the end of the game as compared to the actual wording.

We're praying, O God; my ear hears the words in my mouth!

ART: PRAYER SHAWLS

Materials
one 4-by-1-foot length of white cotton material per child, colored fabric paints, colored fabric crayons, sequins, beads, other decorations, fabric glue, sixteen 1-foot strands of colored yarn per child, four 6-inch strands of off-white yarn per child, small plastic sandwich bags, darning needles with large eyes, stencils of Christian symbols (for example, cross, flame, star, rainbow), scissors

Preparation
1. Put sixteen strands of colored yarn into a sandwich bag. Make one bag per child.
2. Cut four strands of off-white yarn per child.

Directions
1. Give each child a piece of white cotton material.

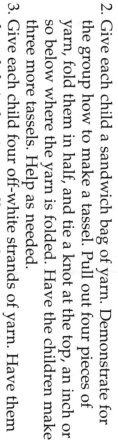

BULLETIN BOARD: HEAR OUR PRAYER, O LORD

Materials

blue paper for background, construction paper, letter stencils or dye cut machine, stapler or pushpins, dark brown paper, leaves cut from green paper (or fall colors if you do this project during autumn), black felt markers, scissors, a copy of your church prayer list

Preparation

1. Cover the board with blue paper.
2. Create a large tree trunk out of dark brown paper. Attach it to the board with staples or pushpins.
3. Create a leaf pattern and cut leaves from the green or fall-colored paper.
4. Use letter stencils or dye cut machine to make the title HEAR OUR PRAYER, O LORD. Attach the title to the board.

Directions

1. Give each child several leaves.
2. Have the children use markers to print a name from the prayer list on each leaf. Divide list as needed among the children.
3. Attach the leaves to the branches of the tree.

HEAR
OUR
PRAYER,
O LORD!

---

2. Give each child a sandwich bag of yarn. Demonstrate for the group how to make a tassel. Pull out four pieces of yarn, fold them in half, and tie a knot at the top, an inch or so below where the yarn is folded. Have the children make three more tassels. Help as needed.
3. Give each child four off-white strands of yarn. Have them thread their darning needles with one strand of yarn and sew a tassle to one of the corners of the material. Repeat until all four tassles are sewn to the corners.
4. Tell the children to decorate their prayer shawls using the fabric paints, fabric crayons, sequins, beads, and so on. They can create their own designs or use the stencils.
5. Let these dry, and afterwards the children may wear the shawls when they pray.

ART: PRAYER SHAWLS ⇦

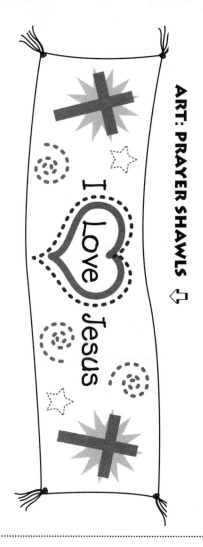

I Love Jesus

PROJECT: PRAYER SERVICE

Help the children plan and present a short prayer service. This can become a part of congregational worship or be a separate service that includes a simple meal. Open the prayer service by singing "Day by Day." Next, say the Lord's Prayer together and invite people to share joys and express concerns that they would like to pray for. Let the children tell about prayer shawls.

PUZZLE: HELLO GOD!

1=A 4=D 7=G 10=J 13=M 16=P 19=S 22=V 25=Y
2=B 5=E 8=H 11=K 14=N 17=Q 20=T 23=W 26=Z
3=C 6=F 9=I 12=L 15=O 18=R 21=U 24=X

__ __   __ __ __ __   __ __ __ __ __ __   __ __ __ __ .
8   5   1 18 13 25 16 18 1 25 5 18 15 7 15 4

__ __ __ __   __ __ __   __ __   __ __ __   __ __ __ __ .
7   9 22 5   5   1 18   20 15   20 8 5   23 15 18 4

__ __   __ __   __ __ __ __ __
15   6   13 25   13 15 21 20 8

From *Bible Verse Fun with Kids.* Copyright © 2004 by Cindy Dingwall. Reprinted by permission.

Chapter 6

HIGH HOPES

But I will hope continually, and will praise you yet more and more.

—Psalm 71:14

PROGRAM

GAME: KITES FOR GOD (See page 32.)

DISCUSSION

Discuss what the word *hope* means. What kinds of things do we hope for? Talk about what having hope in the Lord means. Ask the children to tell you ways they can praise God.

BIBLE STORY

Choose a favorite Bible story that depicts people sharing hope in God. Be creative in how you share the story, for example, flannel board, story cards, puppets, and so on.

SONG: "HOPE IN THE LORD"

("*Row, Row, Row Your Boat*")

Hope, hope, hope, in the Lord! Hope in him always!
Praise, praise, praise the Lord, now and every day!
Hope, hope, hope, in the Lord! Hope in him always!
Praise, praise, praise the Lord, now and every day!

(Once the kids know this, divide them into two groups, and let them sing it as a round.)

SOMETHING SPECIAL

Spirit of Hope by Bob Graham
A family refuses to give up hope when they learn they must move out of their beloved home.

A Child's Book of Hope by Jean Monrad Thomas
Hope is everywhere we look.

ART: BEADS OF HOPE

(See page 32.)

PROJECT: SHARING HOPE

Make Beads of Hope necklaces to send to victims of recent tragedies (see Art, page 32.). Have the children make cards to include with the necklaces.

ACTIVITY: FLYIN' HIGH (See pages 32-33.)

BULLETIN BOARD: WE HAVE HIGH HOPES! (See page 33.)

WORSHIP TIE-IN: OUR HOPE IS IN THE LORD

Help the children write a litany that includes the line "Our hope is in the Lord." Let them think of things they hope for: world peace, kindness, love for all people. Let them share this during congregational worship.

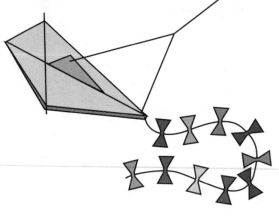

GAME: KITES FOR GOD

Materials

brightly colored construction paper, thick black marker, colored crepe paper for kite tails, clear book tape, glue

Preparation

1. Create a kite pattern. Make 13 kites from colored paper. Attach crepe paper for tails.
2. Print one word of the Bible verse Psalm 71:14 on each kite with black marker.

Directions

1. Give each child a kite.
2. Have the children arrange the verse in the correct order. Attach the kites to the wall or bulletin board.

Directions

1. Give each child a piece of leather. Tape one end to the table. Have the children put five colored beads on the leather strand.
2. Tell the children to slip the letter H onto the leather strand. Add two colored beads.
3. Next, add the letter O, and so until you have added the letter E.
4. Add five colored beads.
5. Assist the children in untaping the end of the leather strand, being careful not to let the beads slip off. Firmly tie the ends of the leather strands together. Let the children wear their necklaces.

ART: BEADS OF HOPE

Materials

one 24-inch length of thin leather per child, letter beads that spell the word HOPE for each child, colorful beads, masking tape, cupcake tins, margarine tub with lid for each child

Preparation

1. Put one H, O, P, and E bead into each child's margarine tub. Close the lid.
2. Divide the colored beads by colors and place into cupcake tins.

ACTIVITY: FLYIN' HIGH

Materials

1 inexpensive easy-to-assemble paper kite per child, one 4-by-6-inch colored unlined index card per child, 1 roll of kite string per child, tape, scissors, postage stamps

Preparation

1. Assemble the kites.
2. Make postcards from the index cards. Put the church address on the front. On the back write the Bible verse Psalm 71:14 and this message: *We have high hopes at ___ (Church Name). Come visit us. Sunday school is at (time) and worship is at (time). Please bring this card with you and give it to an usher. Or add your own message and mail it back to us at church. Thank you. Love, (the 5th and 6th graders or other group name)*

Directions

1. Give each child a postcard. Let them sign their first name and add a postage stamp.
2. Distribute the kites. Tape the postcard to the kite.
3. Give each child a roll of kite string. Help the children attach the string to their kites.
4. Go outside and fly the kites. Take a pair of scissors outside.
5. When the kites get really high, cut the string and let them fly free. Be on the lookout for new visitors to your church or for how many postcards are returned.

Materials

white paper for background, blue, green, purple, white, and black powdered tempera paints, painting sponges, the kites from the "Kites for God" game (see page 32), letter stencils or dye cut machine, red, yellow, and white construction paper, stapler or pushpins, white batting for clouds, scissors, disposable pie tins

Preparation

1. Use the pie tins to mix the different colors of paint. Mix the paints so they are quite thick and won't run. For light blue, begin with white and slowly add blue paint. For dark blue, begin with blue and slowly add black. Mix blue and green and blue and purple together to get several different shades of blue.
2. Set up several tables for the large sheet of white background paper.
3. Cut the white construction paper into cloud shapes. Glue the batting to the paper so the clouds look fluffy. Let dry.
4. Make a large sun from the yellow paper.

BULLETIN BOARD:
WE HAVE HIGH HOPES! ⇦

Directions

1. Let the kids sponge paint the white paper blue to make a brilliant blue sky. Let it dry.
2. Attach the sky to the bulletin board. Next, attach the sun and clouds.
3. Attach the kites from the "Kites for God" game to the bulletin board, so they spell out the Bible verse Psalm 71:14.
4. Make a sign that says WE HAVE HIGH HOPES with letter stencils or a dye cut machine. Attach it to the board.

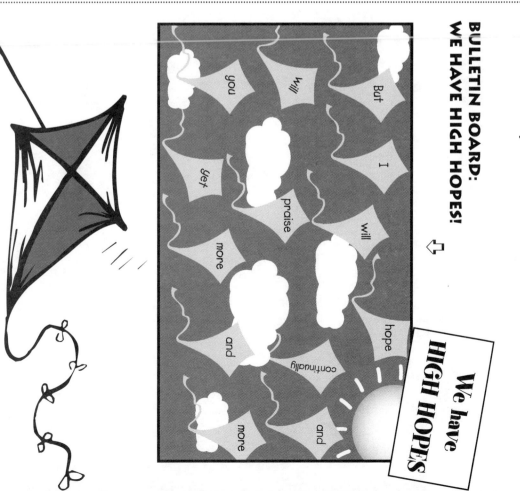

We have HIGH HOPES

Kite words: But I will hope continually yet and praise you more will and more

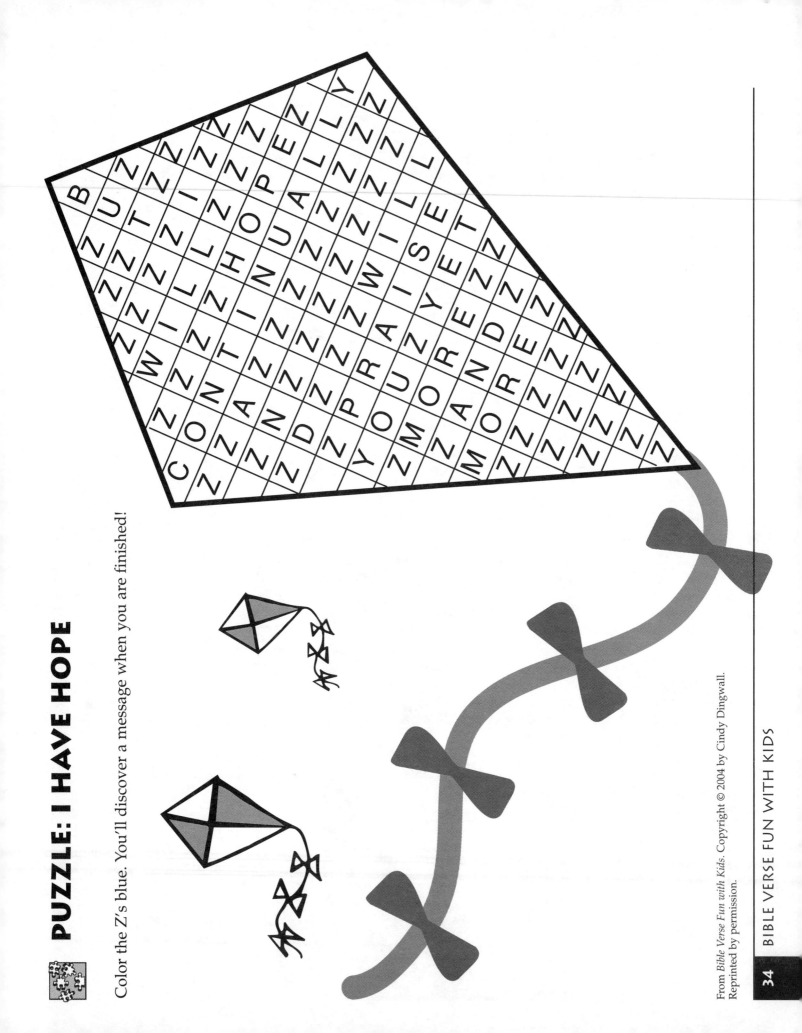

PUZZLE: I HAVE HOPE

Color the Z's blue. You'll discover a message when you are finished!

From *Bible Verse Fun with Kids*. Copyright © 2004 by Cindy Dingwall. Reprinted by permission.

Chapter 7

SING TO THE LORD

O sing to the LORD a new song, for he has done marvelous things.

—Psalm 98:1

PROGRAM

GAME: MUSICAL BALLOON POP

(See page 36.)

BIBLE STORY: PSALM 98

Have children sing and play rhythm instruments as you read the psalm aloud.

DISCUSSION

Ask: Why does God like to hear us sing? How does God feel when we sing?

SONG: "AND I WILL SING"

("Miss Mary Mack")

Teach this as an antiphon. You sing the first phrase; the kids repeat it back to you. Once they know it,

---

SOMETHING SPECIAL

SONG: "Sing, Sing a Song" by Joe Raposo (from *Sesame Street*)

Teach the children to sing this delightful song. Make three colorful cards for the word SING. Choose three children to hold the cards up high whenever they sing the word SING. Music found in *The Sesame Street Songbook.* (See bibliography.)

---

divide the children into two groups. The first group sings the phrase, the second group repeats it. Then switch sides. Let Group 2 sing the phrase while Group 1 repeats it. You can use the SING cards for this song too.

> And I will sing!
> (And I will sing!)
> Sing to the Lord!
> (Sing to the Lord!)
> For he has done!
> (For he has done!)
> Marvelous things!
> (Marvelous things!)

(Vary the tempo. Begin at regular speed. Keep going faster and faster. Then slow it down until you are singing slowly, then go fast again.)

SOMETHING SPECIAL

The First Song Ever Sung by Laura Krauss Melmed
A young boy learns about the first songs ever sung.

My Mama Sings by Jeanne Whitehouse Peterson
When his mother can't find the right song to sing, her son finds just the right one.

ART: SINGING NOTES (See page 37.)

ACTIVITY: GOD LIKES TO HEAR US SING

Have the children use an electronic concordance to discover how many times the Bible tells us to sing. Ask: What does the Bible say to sing about? How many references can you find in the Old Testament (the Psalms, the New Testament) that encourage us to sing?

PROJECT: MUSIC PROGRAM

Teach the children some simple Christian songs ("Jesus Loves Me," "I Am a Sunbeam," "I Will Make You Fishers of People," and so on). Invite children who are proficient on musical instruments to play them on the piano, flute, horn, violin, and so on. Create and practice a short program. Share the musical program with residents at a nearby nursing home. Ask permission from the staff to take treats, for example, cookies and juice, for everyone to enjoy afterwards. Allow time to visit with the residents.

BULLETIN BOARD: WE SING TO THE LORD

(See page 37.)

WORSHIP TIE-IN: LET US SING!

Invite the children to sing some of the songs they know for congregational worship.

GAME: MUSICAL BALLOON POP

Materials

14 large colored balloons, 14 strips of paper, 1 chair per child, joyful children's Christian cassette or CD and cassette or CD player, masking tape, marker

Preparation

1. Print one word of the verse Psalm 98:1 on each strip of paper.
2. Slip a piece of paper with a word into the balloon and blow it up.
3. Set up the chairs for musical chairs. Tape one balloon to one of the chairs.

Directions

1. Have the children form a circle around the chairs. Play the music. When the music stops, everyone must sit on a chair. The child in the balloon chair takes a balloon and pops it by sitting on it. That child will leave the circle and hold on to the strip of paper with the word on it. Remove a chair.
2. When all of the children have popped a balloon and found a word, ask them to put the words into the correct order to reveal the Bible verse.

ART: SINGING NOTES

Materials
1 large wooden musical note per child (purchased or made from plywood), colorful acrylic paints, 2 paintbrushes per child, decoupage solution, 1 copy of the verse Psalm 98:1 per child, pattern for a large musical note, yarn, hammer, nail, clear contact paper

Preparation
1. Use a hammer and nail to poke a hole into the top of each wooden note. String a 6-inch strand of yarn through each note.
2. Type the Bible verse and place it in a circle large enough to fit the wooden notes. Make copies, cut them out, and cover both sides with clear contact paper.

> O, sing to the Lord a new song, for he has done marvelous things.
> —Psalm 98:1

Directions
1. Let each child paint his or her note. Let the notes dry.
2. Give each child a copy of the Bible verse. Let the children cover the note with decoupage solution. Stick the verse onto the note. Cover it with more decoupage solution. Let dry. Suggest that students hang their notes in a window.

IDEA
Take an instant photo of each child or ask the children to bring a wallet sized school photo. Cut the photo into a circle and cover it with clear contact paper. Let the children decoupage their photo to the back of the musical note.

BULLETIN BOARD: WE SING TO THE LORD

Materials
a variety of colored sheets of paper, photos of the kids singing, black construction paper, stapler or pushpins, letter stencils or dye cut machine

Preparation
1. Attach the colored sheets of paper to the bulletin board so it resembles a patchwork quilt.
2. Cut out the title WE SING TO THE LORD from black construction paper. Attach the title to the board.
3. Cut musical notes out of the black construction paper. Attach the musical notes to the board.
4. Take pictures of the children singing during activities, programs, congregational worship, or at the nursing home or retirement center.

Directions
Use pushpins to attach the pictures to the board.

PUZZLE: WHAT SHOULD I DO?

The words inside the half notes (♩) spell out a message for you. Print the message in the spaces below.

TRUTH OR CONSEQUENCES

Chapter 8

I have chosen the way of truth; I have set my heart on your laws.

—Psalm 119:30 NIV

PROGRAM

GAME: CONCENTRATE ON THE TRUTH
(See page 40.)

STORY: "THE BOY WHO CRIED WOLF"
Tell this story to the children. Discuss what happens when we tell lies instead of the truth.

BIBLE STORIES: I TELL YOU THE TRUTH
Use a concordance to look up the word *truth*. In the Gospels there are many instances where Jesus says, "I tell you the truth." Choose any of these statements to share.

DISCUSSION
Talk about why it is important to tell the truth. Remind the children that once we know the truth, we are responsible for the truth. Discuss the consequences of not telling the truth.

SONG: "IF YOU WANT TO TELL THE TRUTH"
("If You're Happy")

If you like to tell the truth shout, "I DO!" (I DO!)
If you like to tell the truth shout, "I DO!" (I DO!)
If you like to tell the truth, if you like to tell the truth, if you like to tell the truth shout, "I DO!" (I DO!)

If you hate to tell a lie, stomp your feet! (STOMP! STOMP!)
If you hate to tell a lie, stomp your feet! (STOMP! STOMP!)
If you hate to tell a lie, if you hate to tell a lie, if you hate to tell a lie stomp your feet! (STOMP! STOMP!)

It is good to tell the truth, oh yeah! (OH YEAH!)
It is good to tell the truth, oh yeah! (OH YEAH!)
It is good to tell the truth, it is good to tell the truth, it is good to tell the truth, oh yeah! (OH YEAH!)

ART: TRUTH PLAQUES
(See pages 40-41.)

PROJECT: THE TRUTH IS . . .
(See page 41.)

ACTIVITY: DO YOU KNOW WHAT'S TRUE? (See pages 41-42.)

SOMETHING SPECIAL

A Big Fat Enormous Lie by Marjorie Weinman Sharmat
That lie just kept getting bigger and bigger!

The Berenstain Bears and the Truth by Stan and Jan Berenstain
The bears have to tell the truth after they have done something wrong.

I	2	chosen	4
	6	truth	8
9	set	11	♥
on	14	15	Psalm 119:30

SAMPLE OF GAMEBOARD WITH GAME IN PROGRESS

I	have	chosen	the
way	of	truth	I
have	set	my	heart
on	your	laws	Psalm 119:30

SAMPLE OF GAMEBOARD WITH VERSE

star, rainbow, moon, tree, heart, and dove. Laminate the cards or cover them with clear contact paper. You should have two cards for each picture.

4. Lay the cards on top of the game in numerical order. The Bible verse should be completely covered.

Directions

Let the first child choose two numbers. Turn over each card. If the pictures on the back match, the child gets to keep the cards. If the numbers do not match, both cards must be placed back on the board.

The next child gets a turn. Keep playing until the Bible verse is revealed. Read it together and discuss it.

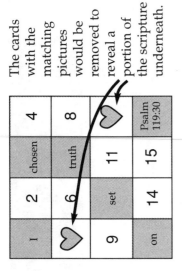

ART: TRUTH PLAQUES

Materials

one 4-by-6-inch wooden plaque per child, acrylic paints in bright colors, disposable pie tins, several sponges per color, 1 copy of the Bible verse Psalm 119:30 per child, clear contact paper, decoupage glue, 1 paintbrush per child, picture hangers

---

BULLETIN BOARD: TRUE OR FALSE

(See page 42.)

WORSHIP TIE-IN: TELL ME THE TRUTH

Gather the children around the altar and ask them the difference between a lie and the truth. Make a variety of statements—some true, some false. Let the children determine which are true or false. Now tell them you are going to make statements that Jesus might or might not have said. Ask: Which ones are true? Which are false?

GAME: CONCENTRATE ON THE TRUTH

(This is similar to the game Concentration.)

Materials

4-by-4-foot game board, sixteen 12-inch square white cards, thick black marker, colored markers, laminating film and machine or clear contact paper

Preparation

1. Print the Bible verse Psalm 119:30 on the game board using thick black marker. If desired, you can outline some of the letters in bright colors or add pictures to the game board. Laminate the game board or cover it with clear contact paper.

2. Number the front side of each card 1 through 16 (See illustration).

3. Draw the following pictures on the back of two cards each: sun, cross,

1	2	3	4
5	6	7	8
9	10	11	12
13	14	15	16

SAMPLE OF GAMEBOARD WITH NUMBERS COVERING VERSE

Preparation

1. Type and print 1 copy of the verse per child. Cover it with clear contact paper.
2. Attach a picture hanger to the back of each plaque.

Directions

Give each child a wooden plaque and have him or her sponge paint it. Once the plaques are dry, give each child a copy of the Bible verse and a paintbrush. Use the decoupage solution to attach the verses to the plaques. Let these dry.

I have chosen the way of TRUTH; I have set my heart on your laws.
Psalm 119:30 NIV

3. Put some liquid dishwashing detergent in the paint so it adheres to the box. Let the children paint the box. When dry, decorate the box with material swatches, sequins, glitter, feathers, and so on.
4. Make a large sign that will stand next to the box that reads: "THE TRUTH IS MANY PEOPLE IN OUR COMMUNITY DO NOT HAVE THE THINGS THEY NEED. Please help us fill their needs by filling this box with shampoo, conditioner, shaving cream, razors, body lotion, soap, toothpaste and toothbrushes. We will take it to the homeless shelter or the food pantry for distribution. Thank you from the kids in our Sunday school program."
5. Consider making this an ongoing service project.

PROJECT: THE TRUTH IS . . . .

Materials

1 large empty box, tempera paint and paintbrushes, liquid dishwashing detergent, fabric swatches, glitter, sequins, feathers, and other decorations, glue

Directions

1. Tell the children: "The truth is that some people don't have everything they need to have." Ask the children if they have soap, shampoo, body lotion, toothpaste and a toothbrush at home, and where they got these things.
2. Start collecting these items from members of the congregation. Encourage people to save toiletries (shampoo, conditioner, body lotion, bars of soap, and so on) from business and pleasure trips. These items can also be purchased in travel sizes.

ACTIVITY: DO YOU KNOW WHAT'S TRUE?

Materials

1 large soup pot, colored index cards, colored markers, wooden spoon

Preparation

1. Write a true or false statement on each card. Include statements that are obvious as well as some statements that the children will have to think about and discuss. Also include true or false questions regarding Bible lessons. Ideas:

Jenna has purple hair.
David has two ears.
Jesus was born in Chicago, Illinois.
Jesus is our Savior.
A friend of yours has no lunch money. You saw her steal another child's lunch. Your teacher asks you if you saw her steal the lunch. Is it okay to tell a lie and say you didn't?
Patrick was teasing Lisa on the playground. He made her cry.

Your teacher asks you what happened. Is it okay to say, "I don't know. I wasn't there"?

2. Put the cards into the soup pot.

Directions

1. Use spoon to stir the pot.
2. Pull out one card at a time and discuss what it says.

BULLETIN BOARD: TRUE OR FALSE

Materials

colored index cards, hole punch, colored markers, self-stick hooks, large sheets of colored paper for a background and lettering, letter stencils or dye cut machine, pencils, scissors, stapler or pushpins, container for the index cards

Preparation

1. Cover the bulletin board with colored paper.
2. Cut out letters that spell TRUE and FALSE. Attach them to the bulletin board.

IDEAS

+ Contribute some true and false statements of your own.
+ Invite members of the congregation to enjoy the TRUE OR FALSE board.
+ Ask members of the congregation to add statements that can be used on the board.

3. Attach the self-stick hooks to the board. Place some under TRUE and others under FALSE.
4. Punch holes in the index cards so they can hang from the hooks.

Directions

1. Encourage the children to think of statements that are true. Let each child write a true statement on one index card. Next, encourage them to think of statements that are false. Let each child write a false statement on one index card. These can be a variety of statements about Jesus, God, Bible stories, Bible characters, and lessons and values the Bible teaches.
2. Put the cards into the container.
3. Take turns pulling the cards out of the container and hanging them from hooks under the correct heading, TRUE or FALSE.

TRUE — God loves me, Jesus is the Savior, Jesus is God's Son
FALSE — Martha was Jesus' mom, It's OK to steal

BULLETIN BOARD: TRUE OR FALSE ⇧

PUZZLE: TELL ME THE TRUTH

Circle the numbers of the statements that are true. You might want to use your Bible to help you. All of the statements are from the NIV Bible translation. When you have found all of the true statements, go back and look for the words that are circled. Write the circled words in the spaces below. They will spell out a message for you to remember.

1. (I) will hasten and not delay to obey your commands. (Psalm 119:60)

2. (Jesus) says it is okay to disobey your parents.

3. Jesus says it is okay to be mean to (other) kids.

4. I (have) compassion for these people. (Matthew 15:32)

5. Jesus is glad you have (chosen) to worship him.

6. It is good to tell (the) truth.

7. It is okay to lie to your (parents) so you won't get in trouble.

8. Jesus' (way) is the best way.

9. Jesus is proud (of) you when you obey his commands.

10. You should always tell the (truth.)

11. It's okay to make paper airplanes out of the bulletins and throw them at people in church.

12. If you and Jesus met, he would say, (I) love you."

13. We (have) to learn to obey rules.

14. You should steal candy from a store when you don't have any (money) to pay for it.

15. Then you will know the truth, and the truth will (set) you free. (John 8:32)

16. The Lord is (my) shepherd. (Psalm 23:1)

17. Love the Lord your God with all your (heart) and with all your soul and with all your mind. (Matthew 22:37)

18. You don't need to love the (Lord.)

19. You should be (on) your best behavior when you go to church.

20. It's okay to hit other (kids) and make them cry.

21. (Your) parents are proud of you when you behave properly.

22. It's okay to cheat on tests at (school.)

23. It's okay to steal another kid's (lunch) if you forget to bring your lunch.

24. (Laws) help keep us safe.

25. God says it is okay to be mean to other (people.)

___ ___ ___ ___ ___

___ ___ ___ ___ ___ ___;

___ ___ ___ ___ ___ ___ ___ .

Chapter 9

THE LIGHT OF THE LORD

Your word is a lamp to my feet and a light to my path.
—Psalm 119:105

PROGRAM

GAME: FLASHLIGHTS (See page 45.)

BIBLE STORY: AND GOD CREATED LIGHT

(Genesis 1:3-5, 14-19)

Talk about the lights that God created. Ask: Why did God create sunlight, moonlight, and starlight? How does light help us? What would happen to the earth if there were no light?

DISCUSSION

Discuss the meaning of Psalm 119:105 with the children. Ask them to tell you how God guides them in your life.

SONG: "THY WORD IS A LAMP" by Michael W. Smith and Amy Grant in *The Big Book of Contemporary Christian Favorites.*

ART: SUN CATCHERS (See page 45.)

ACTIVITY: SHADOWS (See page 46.)

PROJECT: LET OUR LIGHT SHINE

Ask children to donate new night-lights. These can be given to nursing homes or retirement homes for residents to use in their rooms at night.

BULLETIN BOARD: I WILL WALK IN THE LIGHT OF THE LORD!

(See page 46.)

WORSHIP TIE-IN: THE LIGHT OF THE LORD

Put several lights into a large, attractive gift bag. Include a flashlight without batteries, a tap light with batteries, and a night-light. During the children's message, pull out the flashlight and ask what it is and what it is used for. Turn it on. Ask: why won't it work? Open it to reveal no batteries. Next, pull out the tap light, and turn it on. Ask: Why does it work? It has batteries. Show the kids the night-light. Ask: Why isn't it shining? It isn't plugged into an electrical outlet. In order to work, these lights need batteries or electricity. Explain that God's love is like having batteries or electricity. With God's love in our lives, we can share love with everyone. The light of God's love in our lives reminds us to do good. Without God's love, our lives become dark and that is when we sin.

SOMETHING SPECIAL

What Would Jesus Do? by Helen Haidle
Share some of the stories in this book, and let the children discuss options for solving the problems.

"A Light to Guide Us" from the book *The Children's Book of Faith* by William Bennett.

GAME: FLASHLIGHTS

Materials

large flashlight, clear contact paper, a bag, masking tape, instrumental cassette or CD and cassette or CD player, white paper, night-light

Preparation

1. Create a pattern for a lightbulb, and make 16 copies on white paper.
2. Print one word of the verse Psalm 119:105 on each light-bulb. Cover with clear contact paper.
3. Put the bulbs into the bag.

Directions

1. Turn out the lights making the room as dark as possible. If the room seems too dark, plug in a night-light.
2. Play the music and let the children move to it. When the music stops, ask the children to stop.
3. Turn on the flashlight. Shine the flashlight beam (God's light) on one child and let him or her reach into the bag and pull out a shape. The child should read the word on the shape and give it to you. Tape the lightbulb to the front of the child's shirt.

4. When all of the light-bulbs are out of the bag and taped to the children, turn the lights back on. The children should arrange themselves so the verse reads correctly.

ART: SUN CATCHERS

Materials

2 black pipe cleaners per child, one 12-inch strand of black yarn per child, 1 piece of waxed paper per child, 1 piece of sturdy card-board per child, colored glue (add food coloring to white glue to make differ-ent colored glue or pur-chase colored glue)

Directions

1. Give each child two pipe cleaners. Let the children bend these into designs that have closed spaces.
2. Attach a piece of yarn to each pipe cleaner design, so that the sun catcher can be hung.
3. Give each child a piece of waxed paper over sturdy cardboard to put under his or her sun catcher.
4. Let the child pour colored glue into each space on their sun catcher. Keep the sun catcher in one place on the waxed paper.
5. Put the sun catchers aside to dry. Let them dry for 24 to 48 hours on each side. Once dry, they can be hung in a window.

ACTIVITY: SHADOWS

Materials

projector, blank wall, Christian children's cassette or CD and cassette or CD player

Directions

1. Beam the projector light onto the blank wall.
2. Have the children sit on the floor facing the wall, but not blocking the light.
3. Play the music. Let the children take turns dancing with their shadows. Try different things. Each child can dance alone. Two or more children can dance together. Encourage the children to be creative in their movements.

IDEA

Dance outside with your shadow on a cloudless, sunny day.

BULLETIN BOARD: I WILL WALK IN THE LIGHT OF THE LORD!

Materials

long string of Christmas tree lights, extension cord, black paper for background, stapler, letter stencils or dye cut machine, yellow paper, scissors, pencil, shiny gold paper, disposable camera

Preparation

1. Take a photo of each child walking. His or her head may face toward or away from the camera—just make sure his or her entire body is in the shot. Choose which side of the bulletin board the light beam will be on and have every child walking in that same direction.
2. Cut out the child in each photo.

Directions

1. Cover the bulletin board with black paper. Add a light beam of yellow paper. String the Christmas lights around the edges of the board. If needed, use an extension cord to plug them in.
2. Use stencils or a dye cut machine to cut letters of the title out of the shiny gold paper. Attach the letters to the board.
3. Give each child the cutout of his or her full-body photo. Have them put their photo on the board so it looks like they are walking in the light beam. They should be walking in the same direction. As children add their photos, invite them to say how they will walk in the light of the Lord.

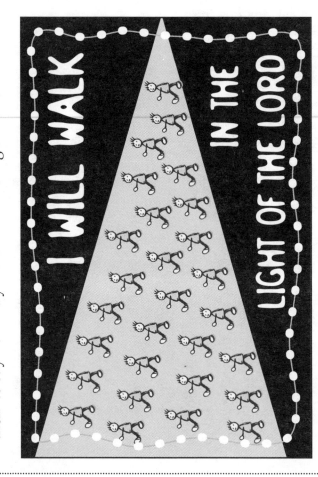

I WILL WALK IN THE LIGHT OF THE LORD

PUZZLE: GOD'S LIGHT GUIDES ME

Use your NRSV or other Bible to look up each Bible verse. Fill in the blanks with the correct word. When you are finished print the words in the spaces below to discover the message.

1. Let the light of ____ ____ ____ ____ face shine upon us, O LORD! (Psalm 4:6)

2. You are my hiding place and my shield; I hope in your ____ ____ ____ ____. (Psalm 119:114)

3. The LORD ____ ____ God, and he has given us light. (Psalm 118:27)

4. Your word is ____ lamp to my feet and a light to my path. (Psalm 119:105)

5. Indeed, you are my ____ ____ ____ O LORD, the LORD lightens my darkness. (2 Samuel 22:29)

6. Be very careful, therefore, ____ ____ love the LORD your God. (Joshua 23:11)

7. The LORD is ____ light and my salvation; whom shall I fear? (Psalm 27:1)

8. My steps have held fast to your paths; my ____ ____ ____ have not slipped. (Psalm 17:5)

9. Your word is a lamp to my feet ____ ____ ____ ____ light to my path. (Psalm 119:105)

10. Arise, shine; for your ____ ____ ____ has come, and the glory of the LORD has risen upon you. (Isaiah 60:1)

11. I hurry and do not delay ____ ____ keep your commandments. (Psalm 119:60)

12. The LORD is ____ ____ shepherd, I shall not want. (Psalm 23:1)

13. Lead me in the ____ ____ ____ of your commandments; for I delight in it. (Psalm 119:35)

____ ____ ____ ____ ____ ____

____ ____ ____ ____ ____ ____

____ ____ ____ ____ ____ ____ ____

____ ____ ____ ____

____ ____ ____ ____

— Psalm 119:105

Chapter 10

PRAISE THE LORD!

Praise the LORD! —Psalm 150:1

PROGRAM

GAME: TICK TACK BIBLE VERSE
(See page 49.)

BIBLE STORY: PSALM 150

Print each verse of Psalm 150 on a large card. Give one card to each child. See if they can arrange themselves in the correct order, so you can read the psalm together. Divide the children into two groups. Have the groups stand facing each other. Let them say the psalm antiphonally. Group 1 will read the first verse together. Group 2 will read the second verse together, and so on until you have read the entire psalm together. Give the children rhythm instruments to use while reciting the psalm. Let them play lutes, harps, strings, pipes, and cymbals as indicated.

DISCUSSION

Discuss why we need to praise God. Ask: How should we praise the Lord? How does God feel when we give thanks and praise? Talk about how we feel when we are praised. Show the children other Bible passages that speak of praising God. Ask: What are ways we can praise God? What can we praise God for?

ART: PSALM PENNANTS (See page 49.)

ACTIVITY: PRAISING GOD! (See page 50.)

SONG: "PRAISE TO GOD!" *("If You're Happy")*

Oh, it's right to give praise and thanks to God!
Oh, it's right to give praise and thanks to God!
Oh, it's right to give praise! It's right to give thanks!
Oh, it's right to give praise and thanks to God!

Let's praise the Lord for our many blessings!
Let's praise the Lord for our many blessings!
Let's give our thanks and praise! Let's give our thanks and praise!
Let's praise the Lord for our many blessings!

(Invite the children to share their praises for God: "Let's praise God for sunny days!" "Let's praise God for our families!" Incorporate their ideas into the song and make new verses to sing.)

PROJECT: PRAISE GOD!

Have the kids make Psalm Pennants to give to people in a nearby retirement center (see Art, this page). When doing this project, omit the pictures of the children.

BULLETIN BOARD: PRAISE THE LORD

(See pages 50-51.)

WORSHIP TIE-IN: PRAISING GOD

Invite the children to share the litany in the "Praising God" Activity (page 50) during congregational worship.

GAME: TICK TACK BIBLE VERSE

Materials

nine 12-inch colored cardboard squares, 9 sheets of white paper, laminating film and machine or clear contact paper, colored broad-tipped felt markers, glue stick, 1 beanbag, masking tape

Preparation

1. Use the colored markers to print one of the following words on each piece of white paper: PRAISE, THE, LORD, TREES, GOD, WATER, ANIMALS, US, FAMILIES.

2. Use the glue stick to attach one word to each colored piece of cardboard. Laminate these or cover them with clear contact paper.

TREES		FAMILIES
THE		
ANIMALS		GOD

**SAMPLE OF BOARD
WHILE GAME IS IN PLAY**

3. Lay the cards on the floor with the words hidden. Arrange the words PRAISE THE LORD so they can be read either down in one line, right to left, or diagonally from top left to bottom right. (See sample.)

4. Mark where the children are to stand to throw the beanbag with masking tape on the floor across from the game board.

Directions

1. Have each child stand behind the masking tape line. Let the children take turns tossing the beanbag at the cards. Turn over the card on which the beanbag lands.

2. Keep playing until the Bible verse Psalm 150:1 is revealed.

TREES	PRAISE	US
WATER	THE	ANIMALS
FAMILIES	LORD	GOD

**SAMPLE OF BOARD
WHEN VERSE IS
REVEALED**

ART: PSALM PENNANTS

Materials

colorful felt, six 12-inch colored ribbons per child, glue, glitter, sequins, one 2-foot dowel rod per child, 1 photo of each child, fabric paints, sewing needle and thread

Preparation

1. Create a pattern of a large pennant on paper. Cut out one felt pennant per child.

Praise the Lord!

2. Glue or stitch the wide end so a dowel rod can be slipped through. The dowel rod should fit in this pocket snugly.
3. Use the needle and thread to stitch around the slots so the pennants will stay on the dowel rods.
4. Take instant photos of each child or ask the children to bring in a school photo from home.

Directions

1. Give each child a pennant.
2. Let them use the fabric paints to write PRAISE THE LORD on their pennants.
3. Have the children decorate their pennants with their photo, sequins, and glitter.
4. Give each child 6 colored ribbons to tie to the top of the dowel rod.

ACTIVITY: PRAISING GOD!

Materials
1 rhythm instrument per child, 1 colored streamer per child

Directions

1. Teach the following litany to the children. Once they learn it, invite them to share it for congregational worship.
2. Let each child think of something to praise God for. See sample below. Your litany will reflect what the kids in your group are thankful for. Let the kids play the instruments after each "Praise the Lord!" response.

All: Praise the Lord!

Child: Praise God for my family!

All: Praise the Lord!

Child: Praise God for my dog!

All: Praise the Lord!

Child: Praise God for our church!

All: Praise the Lord!

Child: Praise God for my grandparents!

All: Praise the Lord!

3. Keep on in this manner until each child has offered praise. End by saying Psalm 150 antiphonally. Let the kids play the instruments as indicated in the psalm. This will be happily and delightfully noisy with the sounds of children praising God! Let the kids toss out streamers at the end of the litany.

BULLETIN BOARD: PRAISE THE LORD

Materials
colored paper for background, colorful gift wrap paper, letter stencils or dye cut machine, stapler or pushpins, candid photos of the children, colored tempera paints, 1 paintbrush per color, soap, water, paper towels, instant camera

Preparation
1. Attach colored paper to the bulletin board for a background.
2. Use the stencils or dye cut machine to make the title PRAISE THE LORD out of gift paper.

Directions

1. Take instant photos of the kids during the program playing, singing, making crafts, and so on.
2. Paint each child's hands a different color. Let the kids make handprints all over colored paper. Let dry and attach as background on the bulletin board.
3. Attach the title and the pictures of the kids to the board.

BULLETIN BOARD: PRAISE THE LORD

↳ *Praise the Lord!*

PUZZLE: SOMETHING TO DO!

You can do all of these things to praise God. As you find each word in the puzzle, cross it out with a yellow crayon or marker. When you have found all of the words, there will be a message for you.

Aim	Walk	Play	Clap	Friendly	Go to church
Ask	Run	Share	Read	Sing	Comfort
Help	Hop	Jump	Learn	Give	Pray

From Bible Verse Fun with Kids. Copyright © 2004 by Cindy Dingwall. Reprinted by permission.

G	O	T	O	C	H	U	R	C	H
I	P	R	A	I	S	E	*	O	*
V	J	C	L	A	P	A	I	M	T
E	U	P	R	A	Y	*	*	F	H
S	M	L	E	A	R	N	W	O	E
I	P	L	A	Y	H	R	A	R	S
N	*	*	D	*	O	U	L	T	H
G	A	S	K	*	P	N	K	*	A
F	R	I	E	N	D	L	Y	*	R
L	O	R	D	H	E	L	P	*	E

Chapter 11

FOLLOW THE STAR

We saw his star in the east and have come to worship him.
—Matthew 2:2 NIV

PROGRAM

 **GAME: FIND THE STAR** (See pages 53-54.)

BIBLE STORIES: THE BIRTH OF JESUS AND THE VISIT OF THE WISE MEN

(Matthew 1:18-25, 2:1-12; Luke 2:1-20)
Both stories will be shared with the children as part of the game, "Find the Star" (pages 53-54).

DISCUSSION

Those portraying Mary and Joseph in the "Find the Star" game can lead this part of the discussion. Remind the children that baby Jesus was born in a stable among the animals. Ask: Why do you think God wanted Jesus to be born in a stable? If Jesus was meant to be king of

all humankind, why wasn't he born in a palace? Why did God put a star in the sky when Jesus was born? Those portraying the Three Wise Men can conduct this part of the discussion. Talk about why it took so long to find Jesus. The wise men can talk about journeying by night and resting by day, so they could follow the star. Let the wise men tell about the gifts they brought to Jesus. Ask the children to share ideas about the gifts they can give to Jesus and to others, for example, love, helping, sharing, and caring.

SONG: "WE HAVE SEEN HIS STAR"
("Twinkle, Twinkle Little Star")

Follow, follow, follow the star.
Worship him whose star we see.
Jesus came to give us light.
Long ago on Christmas night.
Follow, follow, follow the star.
Worship him whose star we see.

ART: CHRISTMAS PLAQUE (See page 54.)

PROJECT: BABY BLANKETS

Ask each family to donate a baby blanket for a child in need in your community.

SOMETHING SPECIAL

They Followed a Bright Star based on a poem by Joan Alavedra. Join the shepherds and wise men as they are led on a journey to Bethlehem.

Come and See by Monica Mayper The shepherds, townsfolk, travelers, and others join in a joyful celebration when Jesus is born.

BULLETIN BOARD: WE HAVE SEEN HIS STAR (See pages 54-55.)

WORSHIP TIE-IN: "WE HAVE SEEN HIS STAR"

Invite the children to sing this song (page 52) during congregational worship.

GAME: FIND THE STAR

This game will lead directly into the story-sharing portion of the program. Ask members of the congregation or high school youth group to assist you. You will need the following characters: Mary, Joseph, Baby Jesus, several Shepherds, and Three Wise Men. The characters in the Living Nativity will be the ones to share the story and lead the discussions.

Materials

one large Christmas star that lights up, cord to use for hanging the star, long extension cord, silver cardboard or aluminum foil, a manger, a large tent, fake straw, stuffed animals for the stable (cow, donkey, birds, and so on), costumes for Mary, Joseph, the Shepherds, and the Wise Men, a doll can represent Baby Jesus if a real baby is not available

Preparation

1. Hang the Christmas star from the ceiling over the manger and plug it into a nearby electrical outlet. Darken the room as

much as possible, so the star glows in the darkness.

2. Set up the tent to resemble a stable. Arrange the fake straw.

3. Cut stars out of silver cardboard, or regular cardboard and cover with aluminum foil. Make a path of cardboard stars along the floor leading to the room where the program is being held.

4. Ask members of the congregation or several youth to portray Mary, Joseph, Jesus, the Shepherds, and the Three Wise Men. Have these characters gather in the room where the program is to be held. Let them surround the manger and wait until the children arrive. Make sure the children do not see your actors prior to the program. The idea is for the children to be surprised when they discover the Holy Family, Three Wise Men, and Shepherds.

Directions

1. Gather the children in an area away from the room where the program will take place. Tell them to follow the stars. As the children arrive in the darkened room, help them notice the star hanging over the manger.

2. Have Joseph ask: "How did you know to come here?" The children can respond: "We followed the stars."

3. Have Mary invite them to sit on the floor while she tells how she found out she was to be the mother of Jesus. Next, have Joseph tell about the journey he and Mary

made to Bethlehem, and why Jesus was born in the stable instead of the inn.

4. The Shepherds can talk about how they were afraid when they saw the bright star in the sky, but followed it to visit Baby Jesus. They can say, "We saw his star in the east and have come to worship him."

5. Have the Wise Men tell how they came to visit Baby Jesus and bring him gifts. They too can say, "We saw his star in the east and have come to worship him."

6. Have the Shepherds or Wise Men ask the children how they came to visit Jesus. Their reply will be, "We saw his star in the east and have come to worship him."

ART: CHRISTMAS PLAQUE

Materials
1 wooden plaque per child (at least 4-by-6-inches), plaque hangers, white paint, paintbrushes, tubes of gold fabric glitter, gold star stickers, decoupage glue, clear contact paper, one box of assorted Christmas cards

Preparation
1. Paint wood plaques with white paint. Let dry.
2. Attach plaques hangers to the back of the plaques.
3. Cut out the front of the Christmas cards so you have only the picture.
4. Cover both sides of the Christmas card with clear contact paper.

Directions
1. Give each child a wooden plaque. Let the children put the gold star stickers around the outside edges.

2. Give each child the front of the Christmas card. Let them glue it to the plaque. Let dry. Children can use these as Christmas decorations at home.

ART: CHRISTMAS PLAQUE ⇧

BULLETIN BOARD: WE HAVE SEEN HIS STAR

Materials
navy blue paper for background, instant camera, large piece of silver cardboard or poster board, pattern for Christmas star, star-shaped sponges, stapler or pushpins, glue, silver glitter, tubes of silver glitter paint, disposable pie tins, white yarn, silver wrapping paper, scissors, white poster board, letter stencils or dye cut machine, construction paper

Preparation
1. Cover the bulletin board with the navy blue paper.
2. Make a pattern for the Christmas star. Cut the star from sil-

ver cardboard or poster board. Cover the star with glue and sprinkle on silver glitter. Let dry. Attach star to the middle of the board.

3. Cut a large cloud out of white poster board.
4. Make the title WE HAVE SEEN HIS STAR! from navy blue construction paper and attach it to the cloud. Use white yarn to hang the cloud from the ceiling.
5. Squeeze the tubes of glitter paint into the pie tins.

Directions

1. Take an instant close-up photo of each child looking up toward the ceiling. Cut out each photo. Set these aside.
2. Let the children sponge paint silver stars on the blue paper. Let dry. Add the Christmas star to the board.
3. Attach the photos of the children along the bottom of the board. The effect should be the children looking up at the stars in the sky.

WE HAVE SEEN HIS STAR

PUZZLE: WHAT'S THAT?

Color the X's dark blue. Color the Z's silver. You'll find a message when you are finished!

Chapter 12

ASK, SEARCH, AND KNOCK

Ask, and it will be given you; search, and you will find; knock, and the door will be opened for you.

—Matthew 7:7

PROGRAM

GAME: FIND THEM! (See page 57.)

DISCUSSION

Talk to the children about always getting what we ask for. Ask: Do you always get everything you ask for? Do you always get everything you want? Is it good to get everything we want or ask for? Why or why not?

Discuss the Bible verse Matthew 7:7. Explain that this is not about getting what we always want, but that God will always be there if we look for God, God will always answer when we call, and that we can find God

SOMETHING SPECIAL

Choose any of the *Where's Waldo?* books by Martin Handford to enjoy with the children. See how long it takes you to find Waldo.

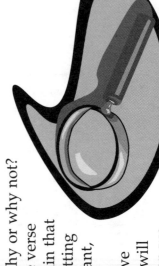

---

wherever we are. Remind the children that God always knows where we are. Unlike the Waldo books we just shared, God can always find us, and we can always find God. Allow the children to share their thoughts on this verse.

BIBLE STORY: THE LOST SHEEP (Luke 15:4-7)

Make this story into a flannel board. Make a background that includes hills, trees, rocks, and so on. Make a bunch of sheep and a shepherd. Hide one of the sheep behind a rock. Tell the story to the children. Explain that God cares enough about us to always know where we are. We can never be lost from God's sight and care. Like a parent, God wants to look after us and keep us safe from harm. Tell the children that we need to look for the right and good things to do. If we ask for God's help, God will help us.

SONG: "SEEK YE FIRST" by Karen Lafferty in *Timeless Praise* by Phillip Keveren.

ART: "SEEK THE LORD" SCROLL
(See page 58.)

PROJECT: SEEK AND YOU WILL FIND
(See page 58.)

BULLETIN BOARD: SEEK IT! FIND IT!
(See page 59.)

WORSHIP TIE-IN:
BEHIND CLOSED DOORS

Make a large poster board with doors. Print something about God or Jesus behind each door. (For example, *You are special. God loves you. Jesus wants you to follow him.*) Invite the children to join you at the altar. Talk to them about doors. Ask: Why do we have doors? What happens when we open doors? Let the kids take turns opening the doors to reveal what is behind them.

GAME: FIND THEM!

Materials

twenty 12-inch square pieces of card stock paper, thick markers, laminating film and machine or clear contact paper, up to 22 older child or adult volunteers

Preparation

1. Cut sheep out of the card stock paper using the pattern on this page.
2. Print one word of the verse Matthew 7:7 on each sheep. Make the words colorful and fun.
3. Laminate each sheep.
4. Assemble up to twenty-two helpers. Give each helper a sheep card and tell them to hide. If you are using fewer than twenty-two helpers, give each person more than one card.

Directions

1. Tell the children that there were some people who agreed to help us with today's lesson, but they disappeared. Ask them to look for the helpers. When

a child finds a helper, he or she must bring them to the center of the room, and tell them to stay there and not go away again.

2. After all of the helpers are assembled, ask them to show their sheep cards. The words will be in random order. Ask the kids to put the helpers in the correct order to display the verse so it can be read properly.

SHEEP PATTERN ⇨

ART: "SEEK THE LORD" SCROLL

Materials

1 cardboard paper towel roll per child, one 2-foot long strand of colored yarn per child, several thin paintbrushes per child, 1 disposable pie tin per paint color, permanent markers, one 2-by-1-foot piece of heavy duty white paper per child, dry tempera paint, 1 cup flour, 1 cup salt, 1 cup water, tape

Preparation

1. Mix 1 cup flour, 1 cup salt, 1 cup water. The mixture should be thick, but have a paintlike consistency. Add small amounts of colored, dry tempera paints to the mixture. Put each color into a different pie tin.

2. Attach the cardboard tube lengthwise to the short end of the long piece of paper. Wrap the paper around the tube and tape it securely, leaving the rest of the paper to hang.

3. Use permanent marker to neatly print the verse Matthew 7:7 on each length of paper.

4. String the yarn through the tube and tie it so the scroll can be hung.

> ASK,
> and it will be given
> you;
> SEARCH,
> and you will find;
> KNOCK,
> and the door will
> be opened for you.
>
> –Matthew 7:7

Directions

1. Give each child a paintbrush and a scroll.

2. Use the paint mixture to paint a border around the verse. Let the scrolls dry. Do not paint on the printed verse.

3. The children can take these home and hang them up.

PROJECT: SEEK AND YOU WILL FIND

Purchase inexpensive reading glasses in different strengths. Explain to the children that some people need glasses so they can see. Let the children try these on and experience having their vision altered.

Tell the children that some families do not have enough money to purchase glasses for their children. Ask them what they think we can do about this. They will come up with several ideas. Encourage the children to think of ways to raise money that can be used to purchase glasses for a child whose family cannot afford them. After you and the children agree upon an idea, put it into action. Ask the congregation to donate glasses they no longer use. These can be donated to a Lions Club in your area who will distribute them to those in need of glasses.

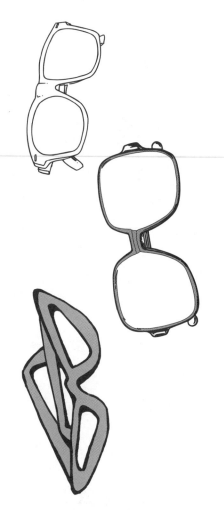

BULLETIN BOARD: SEEK IT! FIND IT!

Materials

multicolored paper, colored construction paper, colored markers, stapler or pushpins, colored magazine photos of a variety of things (colored pictures of Jesus, a door, a hand knocking on a door, someone wearing glasses, a mother and baby, a dad and child, and so on)

Preparation

1. Cover the bulletin board with the multicolored paper.
2. Cut the construction paper into a variety of shapes.
3. Find these photos in magazines and cut them out: colored pictures of Jesus, a door, a hand knocking on a door, someone wearing glasses, a mother and baby, a dad and child, and so on.

Directions

1. Print one word of the Bible verse Matthew 7:7 on each colored paper shape.
2. Make a collage of all of the photos.
3. Hide the pictures of Jesus, the door, the hand knocking on a door, someone wearing glasses, someone looking for something, and so on, among the other pictures to make a

hidden picture puzzle. Hide the words to the Bible verse among the pictures, too.
4. Let children see if they can find the pictures on the list. Invite the congregation to hunt for the hidden pictures.

BULLETIN BOARD: SEEK IT, FIND IT!

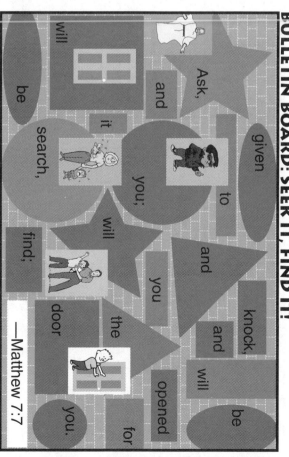

Ask, and it will be given to you; search, and you will find; knock, and the door will be opened for you.

—Matthew 7:7

HINT

Be creative in your use of and placement of pictures in the collage. If necessary, look at a few hidden picture puzzles to guide you in making this large puzzle.

PUZZLE: WHAT CAN WE DO?

Use your pencil to shade the letters of each word as you find it in the row to the right. The letters you don't shade will have a special message.

GOD	A	G	S	O	D	K		
YOU	Y	A	O	N	U	D		
LOVE	I	L	O	V	E	T		
HOPE	H	W	O	I	P	E	L	
FAITH	F	A	B	E	E	T	H	
LORD	G	L	I	O	V	E	R	D	N
LEARN	L	E	Y	A	O	U	R	N
WOW	W	S	O	E	A	W	R	C	H
JESUS	A	J	N	E	S	D	U	S
CREATOR	C	R	E	Y	A	T	O	O	U	R
JOY	W	J	J	I	O	L	Y	L
LOOK	L	F	O	I	O	N	K	D
HELPER	K	H	N	E	O	C	L	K	P	E	R
REDEEMER	R	A	E	N	D	E	E	D	M	E	R
FORGIVES	T	F	H	O	R	G	E	I	V	E	S
KINGDOM	K	D	I	O	N	O	R	G	D	O	M
HAPPY	W	H	I	A	P	L	L	P	Y
SAVIOR	S	A	V	I	O	R	B	E
CARES	O	C	P	A	E	R	N	E	S	D
KING	M	A	K	T	I	H	E	N	W	G
FRIEND	F	S	R	E	I	V	E	N	E	N	D
PRAY	S	E	P	V	R	E	A	Y	D

Chapter 13

KEYS TO THE KINGDOM

I will give you the keys of the kingdom of heaven.
—Matthew 16:19

PROGRAM

GAME: UNLOCK THE MESSAGE (See page 62.)

BIBLE STORY: THE KINGDOM OF HEAVEN

Use a concordance to look up references to the kingdom of heaven in the book of Matthew. Choose the scriptures you want to share with the children. Discuss what Jesus said about entering the kingdom of heaven.

DISCUSSION

Discuss the meaning of the Bible verse Matthew 16:19. What does it mean for God to give us the keys to the kingdom of heaven? Why is it important for us to have the keys of the kingdom of heaven? What are the keys to the Kingdom of heaven? They are sharing, loving, helping, and so on.

ACTIVITY: KEYS TO TREASURES (See page 62.)

SONG: "THE KEYS TO THE KINGDOM" ("The Wheels on the Bus")

The keys to the kingdom are hope and love.
Hope and love, hope and love.
The keys to the kingdom are hope and love.
Hope and love for all!

(Encourage the children to create additional verses.)

ART: KEY CHAINS (See page 63.)

PROJECT: KEYS FOR EVERYONE

Let the children make several key chains (without the three keys from the Art project, page 63.). They can ask members of the congregation to buy them. Let the children decide how the money they raised should be used.

BULLETIN BOARD: THE KEYS TO GOD'S HEART

(See page 63.)

WORSHIP TIE-IN: THE KEY TO GOD'S HEART

Have a large lock and five keys with only one key that will open the lock. Label that key with the word LOVE. Label the remaining keys with the words: HATRED, MEANNESS, SELFISHNESS, DISHONESTY. Give the key labeled selfishness to one of the children, and ask him or her to open the lock. Keep playing until you have one key left—the key labeled LOVE that will open the lock. Let a child open the lock with this key. Explain to the kids that God wants us to show love to one another and that love is one of the keys to the kingdom. Ask them to share ways they can be more loving toward others.

GAME: UNLOCK THE MESSAGE

Materials

1 easy-to-open key ring per child, cardboard, black felt markers, 1 large box that can be locked and unlocked with a key, hole punch

Preparation

1. Make one set of 11 keys per child from cardboard. See pattern on page 64.
2. Print one word of the Bible verse Matthew 16:19 on each of the 11 keys.
3. Punch a hole in the top of each key. Put the keys on the key ring in random order.
4. Put each set of key rings into the box. Lock the box and keep that key in a safe place.

Directions

1. Have the box in view when the children arrive.
2. Ask the children what they think is inside the box.
3. Open the box and reveal the key rings.
4. Give each child a key ring. Have them open the key rings and take the keys off.
5. Ask the children to put the keys in the correct order of the Bible verse and to place the keys back on the key rings in the correct order.

ACTIVITY: KEYS TO TREASURES

Materials

a variety of locks and keys, several locked boxes, candy, toys, stickers, and other prizes, keys to some church rooms

Preparation

1. Make sure some of the keys and locks are similar, so finding the correct key is not too easy.
2. Hide prizes in the locked boxes.

Directions

1. Talk about the different things we lock and why. As a group, unlock several church rooms to discover what is inside each room.
2. Show the children the locked boxes. Let the kids figure out which key opens which box. When they are successful, they keep the treasures inside the box.

ART: KEY CHAINS

Materials

1 key chain with clear plastic holder per child, white card stock paper, 1 copy of the Bible verse Matthew 16:19 per child, colored pencils, three colored metal keys per child, scissors

Preparation

1. Type the verse so that it will fit on the plastic holder. Make one copy for each child.
2. Put three keys on each key chain.

Directions

1. Give each child a copy of the verse. Use the colored pencils to draw a border around the verse and decorate the back side of the paper.
2. Give each child a key chain with the three keys attached, explaining that the keys are to help them remember God the Creator, Jesus the Son, and the Living Spirit.
3. Slip the verse inside the plastic holder.

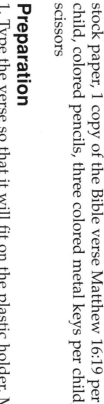

I will give you the keys to the kingdom of heaven.
—Matthew 16:19

BULLETIN BOARD: THE KEYS TO GOD'S HEART

Materials

pink and red construction paper, silver paper, thick red felt tip markers, picture of Jesus, stapler or pushpins, letter stencils or dye cut machine, one 1-by-5-inch strip of white paper per child

Preparation

1. Cover the bulletin board with pink paper.
2. Cut a large heart out of the red paper. Attach the red heart to the center of the board. Put the picture of Jesus in the center of the heart.
3. Create the title from stencils or dye cuts and attach it to the board.
4. Cut one key per child from the silver paper.

Directions

1. Talk about the keys to God's heart: kindness, helpfulness, obedience, and so on.
2. Give each child a strip of white paper and a red marker. Ask them to think of something they will do to show they love God. For example, *Obey my parents. Help my sister. Have them print their choice on the strip of paper.*
3. Give each child a key. Tell them to glue the strip of paper to the key.
4. Have each child attach his or her key to the bulletin board.

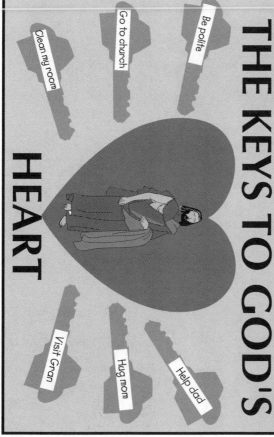

THE KEYS TO GOD'S HEART

Clean my room
Go to church
Be polite
Visit Gran
Hug mom
Help dad

BULLETIN BOARD: THE KEYS TO GOD'S HEART

PUZZLE: SOMETHING FROM JESUS

Connect the letters in the puzzle. Skip the letters C, J, and X! Print the solution on the key.

← start

Chapter 14

FAITHFUL FOLLOWERS

For truly I tell you, if you have faith the size of a mustard seed, you will say to this mountain, "Move from here to there," and it will move; and nothing will be impossible for you.

—Matthew 17:20

PROGRAM

GAME: HIDDEN SEEDS (See page 66.)

BIBLE STORY: THE PARABLE OF THE MUSTARD SEED

(Matthew 13:31-32, Mark 4:30-32)

Ask a male volunteer to dress as and portray Jesus while sharing this parable with the children. Have him show them a mustard seed and a plant that has grown from a mustard seed and discuss how this tiny, tiny seed can grow into a magnificent plant. Explain that even the smallest faith can grow and blossom into something wonderful. Share the meaning of faith, the importance of having a strong faith, and how faith helps us live as good Christians.

> ### HINT
>
> Plant some mustard seeds in a large pot of soil several weeks before this program.

ART: POTS OF BEAUTY

(See pages 66-67.)

PROJECT: SHARING GOD'S BEAUTY

(See page 67.)

ACTIVITY: OUR FAITH STORIES

Share your faith stories with the children. Invite the church member portraying Jesus to share his story as well. Encourage the children to share their faith stories. The children can write their stories or dictate them to an adult.

SONG: "I HAVE FAITH IN GOD"

("Michael Row the Boat Ashore")

I have faith in God,
    Alleluia.
My faith keeps me
    strong, Alleluia.
My faith helps me
    live, Alleluia.
My faith gives me courage, Alleluia.

(*Encourage the children to create additional verses for this song.*)

BULLETIN BOARD: LOOK WHO HAS FAITH (See page 67.)

> ### SOMETHING SPECIAL
>
> *What Happens When Flowers Grow* by Daphne Butler
>   Learn what happens when flowers grow.
>
> *Planting a Rainbow* by Lois Ehlert
>   A mother and child plant seeds that grow into a rainbow of flowers.

GAME: HIDDEN SEEDS

truly

For

you

tell

I

Materials

1 clay pot per child, 1 package of seeds per child (mustard seeds or others you choose), brown paper, markers, scissors

Preparation

1. Cut the brown paper into seed shapes.
2. Print one word of the Bible verse Matthew 16:19 on each seed. Put one "seed" into each empty clay pot.
3. Place one package of seeds into each pot.
4. Hide the pots.

Directions

1. Tell the kids to look for the pots. When the children find one, they keep it.
2. After everyone has found a pot, let the kids figure out the correct order of the Bible verse Matthew 17:20. Have children arrange the seeds in the correct order. Read the verse together.

ART: POTS OF BEAUTY

Materials

1 clay pot per child, 1 package of flower seeds per child, 1 package of mustard seeds per child, white acrylic paint, colored acrylic paints, 1 large paintbrush, 3 or more smaller paintbrushes per paint color, potting soil, several small trowels

Preparation

Paint the pots with white acrylic paint prior to the program.

HINT

Use the pots and seed packages from the "Hidden Seeds" game.

WORSHIP TIE-IN: JUST FOLLOW JESUS

Gather a devil's hat and a Jesus hat. These can be any hats. Ask two adults or members of your youth group to assist. Have one of your helpers wear the devil hat and portray the devil and have the other helper wear the Jesus hat and portray Jesus.

Invite the kids to join you on the altar. Have the devil on one side and Jesus on the other side. Tell the kids we are going to play "Follow the Leader," and they must decide which actions to copy. For example, the devil could make a face while Jesus shakes someone's hand. Who's example will the children follow? Continue with both the devil and Jesus doing actions for the kids to imitate. If a kid follows the devil, he or she must go stand with the devil. When a kid follows Jesus, he or she must go stand with Jesus. If there are any kids with the devil, Jesus and the other kids must do actions worth repeating to get those kids back to Jesus.

Explain that sometimes things or people can tempt us away from Jesus, but standing firm in faith helps us stay with Jesus. When people try to tempt us to do something wrong, we must say, "No way! I won't do that," and walk away. Talk about some things people might do to tempt us. Next, share some things people will do to encourage our faith.

Another way to play the game is to have the kids say, "No way, devil!" when they don't want to follow the devil, and say, "Okay, Jesus!" when they want to follow Jesus.

Directions

1. Give each child a clay pot and have him or her paint pictures and designs on it. Let dry while continuing with the program. After completing the bulletin board, return to this project.

2. Let each child use a trowel to put potting soil into his or her pot.

3. Give each child a packet of seeds to plant. The children can take these home and watch them grow. Remind children that seeds need light and water to grow.

PROJECT:
SHARING GOD'S BEAUTY

Materials

1 clay flowerpot per child, white acrylic paint, colored acrylic paints, several small paintbrushes per paint color, potting soil, annual flowers (geraniums, impatiens, and so on), several small trowels

Preparation

Paint the outside of each pot with white acrylic paint. Let dry completely.

Directions

1. Have the children paint the pots according to the directions above. Let the pots dry while you share a story with the children.

2. Fill the pots with potting soil and transplant some annual flowers in each pot.

3. Ask the pastor or visitation committee to deliver these while visiting hospitalized and home-bound church members.

BULLETIN BOARD:
LOOK WHO HAS FAITH

Materials

colored construction paper, instant camera, candid close-up photos of the children (and adults if desired), stapler or pushpins, letter stencils or dye cut machine, scissors, clear book tape, lined paper (cut to 7 inches by 9 inches), one sheet of colored card stock paper per child (8 1/2 by 11 inches), the Bible verse Matthew 17:20 printed on a piece of paper, glue or glue stick

Preparation

1. Cover the bulletin board with colored paper.

2. Make the title LOOK WHO HAS and attach it to board with staples or pushpins.

3. Attach Bible verse to board.

Directions

1. Use the photos to spell out the word FAITH.

2. Give each child a piece of lined paper. Ask them to write about a time when they had to have faith, for example, before a test, looking for a lost pet, and so on.

3. Glue each faith story to a piece of colored card stock. Attach these around the outside edges of the board.

LOOK WHO HAS

For truly I tell you, if you have faith the size of a mustard seed, you will say to this mountain, 'Move from here to there,' and it will move; and nothing will be impossible for you.
Matthew 17:20

PUZZLE: WHAT DOES GOD WANT US TO HAVE?

Color the boxes with the circles black. Color the boxes with the squares blue. What's the message?

FOR ●	TRULY ■	FOR	I ●	TRULY	I ■
TELL	YOU ●	TELL ●	YOU	IF	HAVE ■
FAITH ■	YOU	HAVE	FAITH ■	SEED ■	THE
SIZE ●	MOVE ■	SIZE	HERE ●	TO ■	THERE ●
MOUNTAIN ●	OF	SEED ■	SAY	A ●	YOU ●
MUSTARD	SEED	SIZE	YOU ●	TO ■	WILL
SAY	THE	TO ■	THIS	MOUNTAIN	FAITH ●
FOR ■	MOVE	YOU ●	MOVE ●	SIZE ■	FROM
HERE ■	I	TO ●	TELL	YOU ■	TO ●
SEED ■	THERE	AND	IT	SAY ●	MOVE ■
WILL	SAY ■	MOVE	I	FOR ■	AND ■
THERE ●	AND ●	MOVE ●	YOU	FOR ●	NOTHING ●
SEED ●	FROM	WILL	TELL	BE ●	I
OF	IMPOSSIBLE ■	FOR	IF ■	YOU ●	YOU ●

Chapter 15

WITH ALL YOUR HEART

You shall love the Lord your God with all your heart, and with all your soul, and with all your mind.

—Matthew 22:37

PROGRAM

GAME: HEARTBEATS (See pages 70-71.)

Tell this story to the children.

BIBLE STORY: THE GREATEST COMMANDMENT

(Matthew 22:34-40)

DISCUSSION

Discuss the Bible verse Matthew 22:37 and the story. What does the verse tell us to do? What do we learn from the story? Why does Jesus want us to do this? Discuss ways we can show our love for God. What happens when we show love? What happens when people don't show love?

SONG: "I LOVE THE LORD!"

("When the Saints")

I love the Lord (touch heart, touch heart,
touch heart, touch heart)
With all my heart (touch heart, touch heart,
touch heart, touch heart)

I love the Lord with all my
heart! (touch heart, touch
heart, touch heart, touch
heart)
I love the Lord with all my
heart! (touch heart, touch
heart, touch heart, touch
heart)
And with my soul and mind
too! (stamp, stamp, clap,
clap)

ART: LOVING HEARTS (See page 71.)

PROJECT: LOVE COOKIES (See page 71.)

BULLETIN BOARD: LOVE THE LORD

(See page 72.)

WORSHIP TIE-IN: GOD HAS A BIG HEART

Have two large pieces of red paper and a pair of scissors. Invite the children to join you on the altar. Give the scissors and one of the

pieces of paper to one of the children. Instruct him or her to cut a hole in the center of the paper that is large enough to allow the paper to fit over at least five kids. They won't be able to do it.

Take your paper and fold it in half. Cut according to the diagram. Open the paper. This time it is large enough to fit over at least five kids. Explain that God's heart is big enough to love and care for everyone in the whole world.

WHEN DONE, YOU SHOULD HAVE A LARGE, PAPER RING THAT CAN FIT A FEW CHILDREN INSIDE IT!

GAME: HEARTBEATS

Materials

glue, scissors, masking tape, laminating film and machine or clear contact paper, one drum, large empty ice-cream container (check with a local ice cream store), red, pink, and white paper, thick pointed black felt marker

Preparation

1. Cover the outside of the ice cream bucket with red paper.
2. Use the black marker to draw a large heart and cut it from the pink and white paper.
3. Draw 24 puzzle pieces on the white heart. Cut them out. Trace each puzzle piece onto the white heart. Laminate the white heart or cover with clear contact paper. Mount the white heart on the wall with tape.

Step 1
large piece of paper
fold in half

Step 2
folded side
cut along dotted lines to the end of the arrows

Step 3
folded side
Your folded piece of paper should have slits, like these.

Step 4
X
Where there are O's, cut apart fold.
Where there are X's, keep folded portions intact.

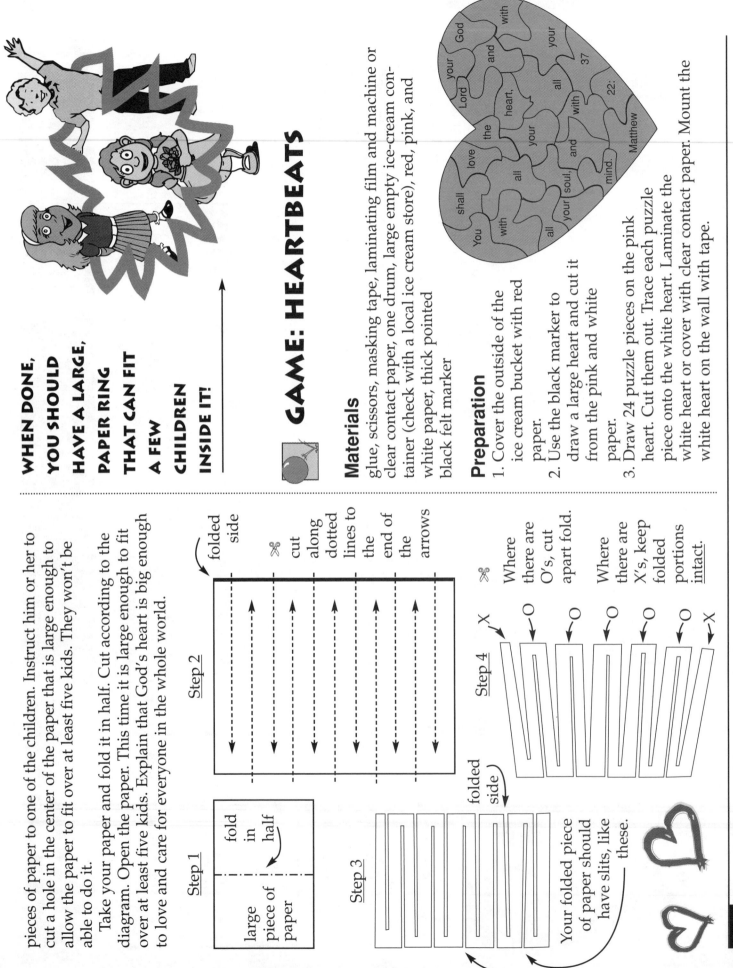

(Heart puzzle text: Lord your God and with your the heart, love all your with 37 shall all your soul, and 22: You with all mind. Matthew)

4. Print one word of the Bible verse Matthew 22:37 on each puzzle piece. Laminate or cover each puzzle piece with clear contact paper. Put the puzzle pieces into the empty ice-cream bucket.

Directions

1. Have the children sit in a circle. Play the drum so it sounds like heartbeats.
2. Tell the children to pass the bucket to the right while the heartbeat plays. When the heartbeat stops, the child holding the bucket will reach in and pull out a puzzle piece. That child will take the piece and attach it with tape to the correct space on the white heart that is mounted on the wall. Keep playing until the pink puzzle is complete. Then read the Bible verse together.

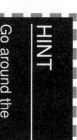

HINT

Go around the circle more than once if you have a small group.

ART: LOVING HEARTS

Materials

1 wooden heart shape per child (purchased or made from plywood), decoupage solution, pink and red acrylic paints, computer generated copies of the Bible verse Matthew 22:37, paintbrushes, red and pink colored pencils, small hammer, picture hangers, scissors

Preparation

1. Paint both sides of each heart pink or red. Let dry.
2. Using a computer, type and print the Bible verse. Draw a heart shape around the verse that is smaller than the wooden hearts. Cut out the hearts making one for each child.
3. Use a hammer to attach the picture hangers to the back of the hearts.

Directions

1. Give each child a heart-shaped Bible verse. Let them use the red and pink pencils to decorate the outside edges of the paper with the verse printed on it. Laminate or cover the verse with clear contact paper.
2. Let children decoupage the Bible verse to the center of the wooden heart. When dry, the children can take them home and hang them in their rooms.

You shall love the Lord your God with all your heart, and with all your soul, and with all your mind.
—Matthew 22:37

PROJECT: LOVE COOKIES

Materials

several batches of sugar cookie dough, cookie sheets, rolling pins, red and pink food coloring, cooling racks, flour, red and pink frostings, gels, sprinkles, oven, Valentine's Day paper plates, pink plastic food wrap, heart-shaped cookie cutters

Directions

1. Let the kids use the rolling pins to roll out the cookie dough. If desired, kids can add red or pink food coloring to the dough they are working with.
2. Use the heart-shaped cookie cutters to cut the cookie dough.
3. Bake the cookies according to the directions, and let cool on the cooling racks.
4. Decorate the cookies using the frostings, gels, and sprinkles.
5. Put an equal number of cookies on each paper plate and cover with the pink plastic food wrap.
6. Deliver the cookies to homebound and hospitalized church members.

HINT

Make heart-shaped cards for people who can't have food treats.

BULLETIN BOARD: LOVE THE LORD

Materials

heart-shaped cookie cutters, white heavy duty paper, disposable pie tins, red thin tipped felt pens, scissors, pencil, stapler

---

or pushpins, shiny red paper, white glue, newspapers, red and pink tempera paints mixed so they are quite thick, letter stencils or dye cut machine, newspaper

Preparation

1. Make the title using stencils or the dye cut machine from the shiny red paper. Glue the letters to the white paper.
2. Mix the tempera paints so they are quite thick.

Directions

1. Let each child dip a cookie cutter into either the red or pink paint. Then let the child make a heart print onto the white paper. They may need to blot the cookie cutters on newspaper before making their prints on the white paper.
2. Let the heart prints dry completely.
3. Let each child use a red marker to write something they would do to show love for others—for example, *share, teach, help, care, pray, befriend, play.*
4. Attach the paper to the bulletin board.

YOU SHALL LOVE THE LORD YOUR GOD WITH ALL YOUR HEART, AND WITH ALL YOUR SOUL, AND WITH ALL YOUR MIND.

care sing pray
play help praise
befriend obey worship

BULLETIN BOARD: LOVE THE LORD ⇧

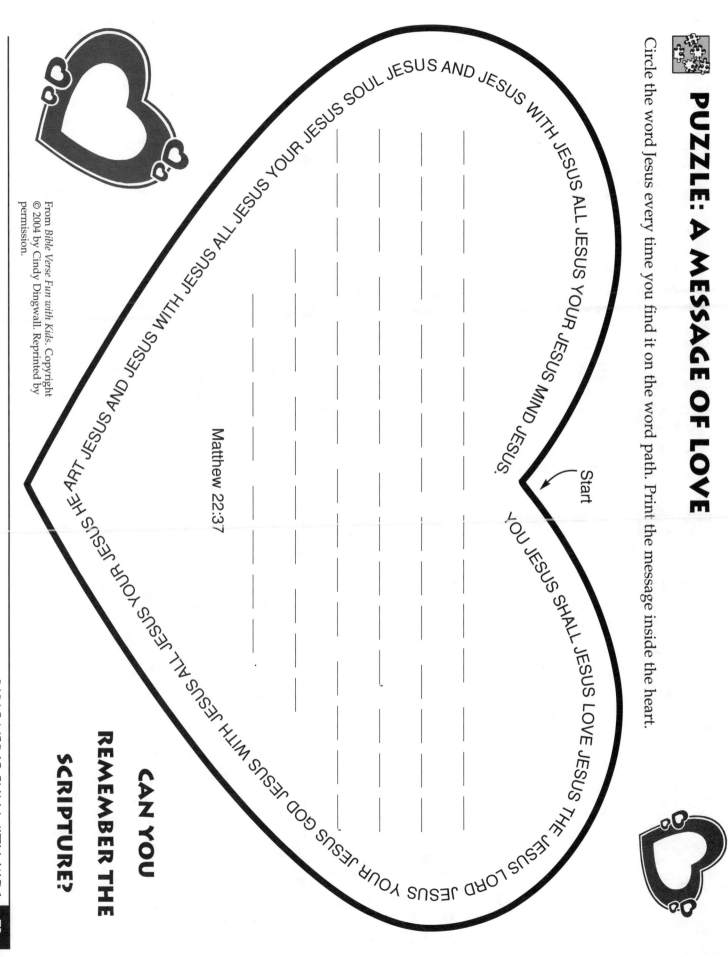

PUZZLE: A MESSAGE OF LOVE

Circle the word Jesus every time you find it on the word path. Print the message inside the heart.

Start

YOU JESUS SHALL JESUS LOVE JESUS THE JESUS LORD JESUS YOUR JESUS GOD JESUS WITH JESUS ALL JESUS YOUR JESUS HE ART JESUS AND JESUS WITH JESUS ALL JESUS YOUR JESUS SOUL JESUS AND JESUS WITH JESUS ALL JESUS YOUR JESUS MIND JESUS.

Matthew 22:37

CAN YOU REMEMBER THE SCRIPTURE?

Chapter 16

PROMISES, PROMISES

And remember, I am with you always, to the end of the age.
—Matthew 28:20

PROGRAM

GAME: JESUS PROMISED (See page 75.)

DISCUSSION

Once the Bible verse Matthew 28:20 has been discovered in the "Jesus Promised" game, explain that this is a promise that Jesus made to us. Ask the children to tell you what a promise is. What does it mean to make a promise? What happens when someone breaks a promise?

BIBLE STORY: THE GREAT COMMISSION

(Matthew 28:16-20)

Tell this story to the children. Talk about the promise that Jesus wants us to make that we will tell everyone about him. Jesus in turn, promises to stay with us always and help us live as Christians.

SONG: "STANDING ON THE PROMISES"

by R. Kelso Carter in *The Big Book of Hymns*

ART: "I AM WITH YOU ALWAYS" DOORHANGER

(See page 75.)

ACTIVITY: LITANY OF PROMISES

(See page 76.)

PROJECT

Make several "I am with you always" doorhangers (page 75). Set a price and sell them to members of the congregation and friends. Identify three organizations in need of financial assistance and let the children decide where to donate the money.

BULLETIN BOARD: JESUS MAKES THE BEST PROMISES!

(See pages 76-77.)

WORSHIP TIE-IN: LITANY OF PROMISES

Invite the children to share the "Litany of Promises" (page 76) during congregational worship.

GAME: JESUS PROMISED

Materials

13 buckets (empty ice-cream buckets from an ice-cream shop), 1 beanbag, 13 index cards, thick black marker, construction paper, stickers, glue

Preparation

1. Decorate the buckets with stickers and construction paper. Print one letter of the words JESUS PROMISED on each bucket.
2. Line up the buckets so they spell JESUS PROMISED.
3. Print one word of the Bible verse Matthew 28:20 on each card.
4. Place the cards in the buckets randomly.

Directions

1. Have the children take turns tossing a beanbag into a bucket. If the beanbag lands in the bucket, he or she can take out the word card.
2. After all cards have been removed, challenge the children to put the verse in the correct order and read it aloud.

HINT

For large groups, set up more than one game and see which group is first to reveal the verse. For smaller groups, kids can have more than one turn throwing the beanbag.

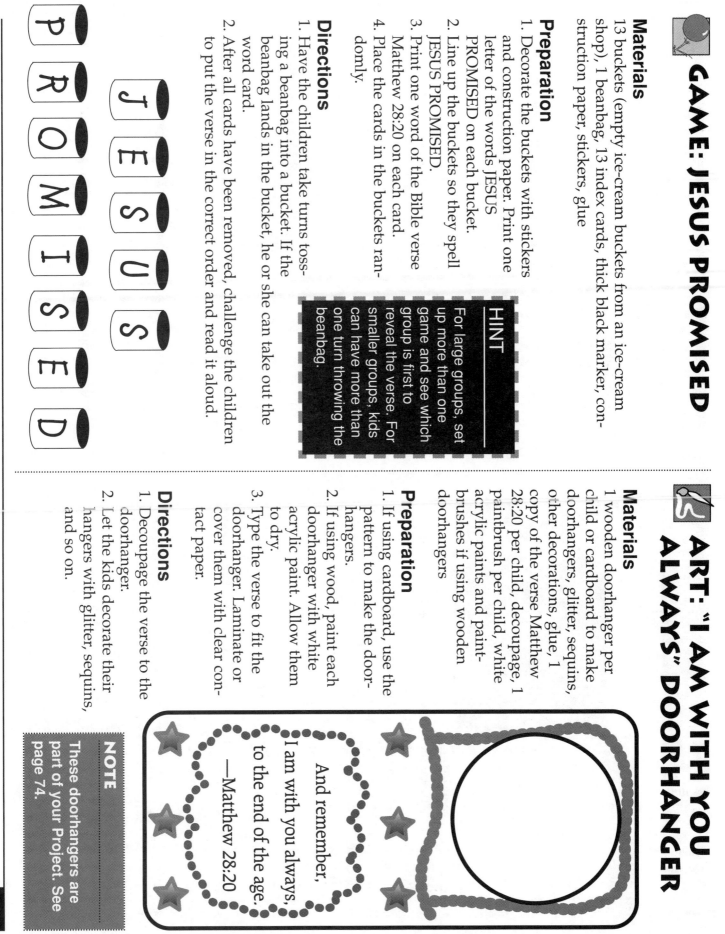

```
J E S U S
P R O M I S E D
```

ART: "I AM WITH YOU ALWAYS" DOORHANGER

Materials

1 wooden doorhanger per child or cardboard to make doorhangers, glitter, sequins, other decorations, glue, 1 copy of the verse Matthew 28:20 per child, decoupage, 1 paintbrush per child, white acrylic paints and paintbrushes if using wooden doorhangers

Preparation

1. If using cardboard, use the pattern to make the doorhangers.
2. If using wood, paint each doorhanger with white acrylic paint. Allow them to dry.
3. Type the verse to fit the doorhanger. Laminate or cover them with clear contact paper.

Directions

1. Decoupage the verse to the doorhanger.
2. Let the kids decorate their hangers with glitter, sequins, and so on.

And remember,
I am with you always,
to the end of the age.
—Matthew 28:20

NOTE

These doorhangers are part of your Project. See page 74.

ACTIVITY: LITANY OF PROMISES

Materials

crayons, white paper

Directions

1. Talk to the children about the promises that Jesus made. Remind them of what it means to make and keep a promise.
2. Encourage the children to think of promises that they can make, for example, *I promise to help my parents with my little sister or brother. I promise not to say bad words.*
3. Let each child choose a promise to make.
4. Give each child a piece of white paper and crayons. Let them write their promise and decorate it.
5. Ask everyone to form a circle and do the following "Litany of Promises."

A Litany of Promises

Leader: Jesus said, "Remember I am with you always, even to the end of the age."

Response: Jesus is always with us.

(Let each child have a turn sharing the promise they are making. After each child has shared his or her promise, respond with "Jesus is always with us.")

Leader: Let us remember what Jesus said: "Remember I am with you always, even to the end of the age."
Response: Let us remember that Jesus is always with us! Hooray!
All: Sing "I Am with You Always" (*"For He's a Jolly Good Fellow"*).

HINT

When sharing the litany during worship, ask the congregation to join in the response. Ask the kids to sing the song once and invite the congregation to sing along with them the second time.

I am with you always!
I am with you always!
I am with you always!
To the end of the age!
To the end of the age!
To the end of the age! I am with you always . . . to the end of the age! Hooray! (*Kids jump up with arms reaching up high.*)

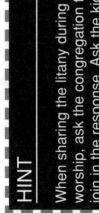

BULLETIN BOARD: JESUS MAKES THE BEST PROMISES!

Materials

white paper, powdered color tempera paints, 3 sponges per paint color, disposable pie tins, large picture of Jesus, colored markers, Bible verses of Jesus' promises, stapler or pushpins, letter stencils or dye cut machine

Preparation

1. Cover the board with white paper.
2. Cut one word cloud per child from white paper.
3. Cut out the letters for the title JESUS MAKES THE BEST PROMISES and attach it to the board.
4. Place Jesus in the center of the board.
5. Mix the tempera paints so they are quite thick and put them into pie tins.

Directions

1. Let the kids sponge paint the white background. Let this dry.
2. Assign each child a Bible verse to look up: Matthew 4:19, Matthew 7:7-8, John 5:24, John 8:12, John 10:9, John 10:11, John 11:25, and other favorites.
3. Give each child a white word cloud and a colored marker. Have them print their verse on their cloud.
4. Use pushpins or staples to attach the word clouds to the board so that they surround Jesus.

BULLETIN BOARD: JESUS MAKES THE BEST PROMISES! ⇨

- Follow me and I will make you fish for people. Matthew 4:19
- I am the light of the world. John 8:12
- I am with you always, to the end of the age. Matthew 28:20
- I am the gate. John 10:9
- I am the resurrection and the life. John 11:25
- I am the bread of life. John 6:48

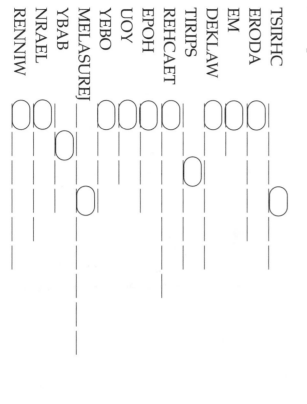

PUZZLE: JESUS PROMISED

Somehow, these words got printed backwards. Can you fix them? Print the correct words in the spaces to the right. Print the circled letters in the spaces at the end to discover what Jesus promised.

TSIRHC

ERODA

EM

DEKLAW

TIRIPS

REHCAET

EPOH

UOY

YEBO

MELASUREJ

YBAB

NRAEL

RENNIW

RETSAE

YRAM

SUSEJ

SAMTSIRHC

ROIVAS

HTURT

DREHPEHS

REGNAM

TSAEF

NEVAEH

DOG

YEKNOD

REHTAF

RATS

PLEH

MEHELHTEB

SELCARIM

DOOG

EGARUOC

"_____ _____ _____, _____ _____." (Matthew 28:20)

From *Bible Verse Fun with Kids*. Copyright © 2004 by Cindy Dingwall. Reprinted by permission.

Chapter 17

LOVE YOUR NEIGHBOR

You shall love your neighbor as yourself.

—Mark 12:31

PROGRAM

GAME: I'M PUZZLED (See page 79.)

BIBLE STORY: THE GOOD SAMARITAN
(Luke 10:25-37)

Tell this story to the children. Ask: How did each of the characters feel? What would you do if faced with this situation? Next, let the children dramatize the story. You'll need children to portray the man walking from Jerusalem to Jericho, several robbers, a priest, a Levite, a Samaritan, and an innkeeper. If you have more children than available parts, assign the remaining children to be villagers. You will be the narrator. Go over each child's part, helping him or her decide what to say and do. Consider presenting this parable during congregational worship.

SONG: "JESUS SAID TO LOVE OUR NEIGHBORS" (*"Michael Row the Boat Ashore"*)

Jesus said to love our neighbors, Alleluia.
Jesus said to love our neighbors, Alleluia.
Jesus said to help our neighbors, Alleluia.
Jesus said to help our neighbors, Alleluia.

ART: GOOD NEIGHBOR AWARD
(See pages 79-80.)

PROJECT: HELPING OUR NEIGHBORS

Talk about how we can help our neighbors. Challenge the children to enlist their parents to help a nearby neighbor, for example, supplying food during an illness, visiting homebound people, running errands, watching children so a mother can do some errands or rest, yard work, and so on. After several weeks have passed, ask each child to report back on what they did to help their neighbor.

BULLETIN BOARD: WE'RE GOOD NEIGHBORS (See page 81.)

WORSHIP TIE-IN: LOVING THOUGHTS

Have a bag of little heart-shaped candies with word messages. Invite the kids to come to the altar. Ask them what love means? How does it feel to give love? How does it feel to receive love? How can we show love to each other? Show the kids the candies. Read some of the silly things they say. Help them think of what they would put on a candy that would tell someone how much God loves them. Give each child a candy to eat.

GAME: I'M PUZZLED

Materials

large colorful poster board, laminating film and machine or clear contact paper, scissors, black felt marker, white paper, large container, glue stick

Preparation

1. Use the black marker to print each word of the verse Mark 12:31 on a piece of white paper.
2. Cut out each word and glue the verse to the poster board.
3. Laminate the poster board or cover it with clear contact paper.
4. Cut the poster board into puzzle pieces. Put the puzzle pieces into the container.

Directions

1. Let each child pull a puzzle piece out of the container.
2. Tell the kids to put the puzzle together and discover the Bible verse.

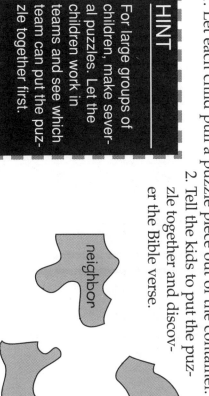

ART: GOOD NEIGHBOR AWARD

Materials

1 certificate per child, crayons or colored pencils

Preparation

Make copies of the certificate. See example on page 80.

Directions

1. Talk about what being a good neighbor means. What do good neighbors do for one another? Explain that we are going to create certificates to give to our neighbors. Tell the children to decide which neighbor they want to thank.
2. Give each child a certificate. Let the children use the crayons or colored pencils to decorate their certificates. Children may add why they are thanking their neighbor in the space provided.
3. Let the children take their certificates home and give them to their favorite neighbors. If desired, the children can make more than one certificate or you may provide additional certificates for them to take home to decorate and give to their neighbors.

Good Neighbor Award

This certificate is awarded to

for being a GOOD NEIGHBOR on this day _____

Thank you for _____

Signed by: _____

Good Neighbor Award

This certificate is awarded to

_____

for being a GOOD NEIGHBOR

on this day _____

Thank you for _____

Signed by: _____

BULLETIN BOARD: WE'RE GOOD NEIGHBORS

Materials

yellow and red construction paper, colored felt markers, photos of different places in your neighborhood, large photo of your church, photos of the children or an instant camera, stapler or push-pins, letter stencils or dye cut machine

Preparation

1. Cover the board with yellow construction paper.
2. Cut out the letters for the title WE'RE GOOD NEIGHBORS from red paper and attach them to the board.
3. Take instant photos of the children or ask them to bring photos from home.
4. Take instant photos of places in your neighborhood, for example, fire station, police station, hospital, children's homes, stores, and schools.
5. Enlarge a photo of your church.

Directions

1. Show the photos of places in your neighborhood to the children. Talk about how each of these places is a good neighbor.
2. Discuss how we can be good neighbors. Talk about how the church can be a good neighbor.
3. Put the picture of your church in the center of the bulletin board. Add the pictures of the other places in your neighborhood.
4. Add the pictures of the children.

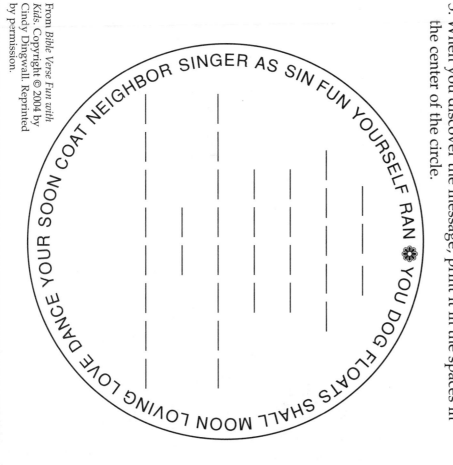

PUZZLE: LOVE GOES AROUND

1. Cross out the words that begin with the letter D.
2. Cross out words that have six letters.
3. Cross out words that end with the letter N.
4. Cross out words that rhyme with BOAT.
5. When you discover the message, print it in the spaces in the center of the circle.

SINGER AS SIN FUN YOURSELF RAN ❁ YOU DOG FLOATS SHALL MOON LOVING LOVE DANCE YOUR SOON COAT NEIGHBOR

From *Bible Verse Fun with Kids*. Copyright © 2004 by Cindy Dingwall. Reprinted by permission.

Chapter 18

JOY TO THE LORD

You will have joy and gladness, and many will rejoice at his birth.
—Luke 1:14

PROGRAM

GAME: BALLOONS OF JOY (See page 83.)

BIBLE STORY: JOHN THE BAPTIST

(Luke 1:1-80, 3:21-23)

Tell the story of John's birth to the children. Continue John's story from Luke 3. Tell how he came to baptize people, including Jesus. Ask the children why they think John was the one who did the baptizing rather than Jesus. (*This was God's plan. God created John so he could baptize people.*) Talk about the joy that people feel when they learn they are to become parents. Be sensitive to the different ways children become part of a family (birth, adoption, marriage, and blended families).

Ask the parents to briefly share how their children came to be a part of their family. Talk about the ways children bring joy to their families. Encourage the children to think of specific things they can do that will bring joy to their families. After sharing the story of John the Baptist, go over Luke 1:14 once again. Help the children understand the meaning of the verse after hearing John's story.

SONG: "YOU'LL HAVE JOY!" ("She'll Be Comin' 'Round the Mountain")

You'll have joy when he comes, yes you will!
You'll have joy when he comes, yes you will!
You'll have joy! You'll have joy! You'll have joy! You'll have joy!
You'll have joy when he comes, yes you will!

You'll rejoice at his birth, yes you will!
You'll rejoice at his birth, yes you will!
You'll rejoice! You'll rejoice! You'll rejoice! You'll rejoice!
You'll rejoice at his birth, yes you will!

ART: JOY BOX
(See pages 83-84.)

ACTIVITY: BAPTIZED IN GOD'S LOVE

(See page 84.)

PROJECT: SOMETHING FOR BABY

Ask each child to bring a box of disposable diapers. Donate these to an agency or organization that works with families in need.

BULLETIN BOARD: LOOK WHO BRINGS US JOY! (See page 84.)

SOMETHING SPECIAL

Welcome, Little Baby
by Aliki
A little baby is welcomed to the world by a loving mother.

Someone's Come to Our House
by Kathi Applet
The family was thrilled with the arrival of a new baby.

WORSHIP TIE-IN: A BOX FROM GOD

You will need two boxes, one wrapped in black paper and the other wrapped in shiny gold paper. Make several rocks out of gray paper. Use black marker to print a "sorrow" on the gray rocks, for example, *a bad grade on my report card, a fight with my friend, getting in trouble with mom, being teased by a bully.* Put these rocks into the black box. Make an identical set of rocks. On the new sorrow rocks, write how God turned that sorrow into a joy, for example, *When I got a bad grade on my math test, my teacher offered to help me. When another kid made fun of me, my friends told him to stop.* Now make several colored paper rocks. Print a joy on each rock, for example, *having parents who love me, my friends who help me, teachers who want to help me learn.* Put the remaining sorrow rocks and all of the joy rocks into the gold box.

Invite the kids to join you on the altar. Show the kids the boxes. Tell the children that you have put all of your sorrows into the black box and all of your joys into the gold box. Open the boxes to reveal their contents. The black box will have a few sorrows in it, while the gold box will be overflowing with joys.

Ask the children why the box of joy has more rocks than the box of sorrow. Tell them that God helps us cope with sorrows by loving us and giving us strength, and that our joys multiply when God helps us. Remind them of all of the blessings God gives, and the many joys God places in our lives.

GAME: BALLOONS OF JOY

Materials

14 large colored balloons, colored markers, 14 strips of white paper, 14 long pieces of colored paper.

Preparation

1. Print one word of the verse Luke 1:14 on each strip of white paper.

---

2. Put one strip of paper inside each balloon.
3. Blow up the balloons and attach a ribbon to each balloon.
4. If you have a helium tank, let the balloons rise to the ceiling with the ribbons hanging down. If not, gather the balloons on the floor.

Directions

1. Let each child choose a balloon.
2. Instruct the children to pop their balloons. Let them decide how they will pop it. Enjoy the "joyful noise" made by the popping balloons and shrieking children.
3. Challenge the children to put the strips of paper in the correct order.

HINT

If you have more than 14 children, divide them into groups. Have each group choose a balloon.

ART: JOY BOX

Materials

1 empty shoe box per child, color tempera paints (blue, red, green, purple), paintbrushes, liquid dish washing detergent, glitter, sequins, shells, pictures cut from magazines, glue, an item for you to put into each child's Joy Box (examples: Bible verse card, a note from you telling why you enjoy having him or her in class)

Preparation

1. Mix the tempera paints. Add a small squirt of liquid dish washing detergent to the mix so the paints will adhere to the boxes.

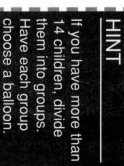

BULLETIN BOARD: LOOK WHO BRINGS US JOY!

Materials

brightly colored paper, white paper, letter stencils or dye cut machine, one photo of each child, colored markers, stapler or pushpins, one strip of paper per child, parents

Preparation

1. Cover the bulletin board with colored paper.
2. Cut out the title LOOK WHO BRINGS US JOY from white paper and attach to board.
3. Write on the strips of paper: _____ (child's name) brings JOY when he [or she] _____.

Directions

1. Ask parents to fill out the strip of paper.
2. Give each child a pushpin, his or her photo, and the strip of paper.
3. Let each child find a place for his or her picture and "joy strip" and pin them to the board.

LOOK WHO BRINGS US JOY!

---

2. Paint each box and let dry for at least 24 hours.
3. Create a Joy Box that includes things that give you joy, (example: photos of friends or family, funny cartoons, inspirational articles, cards sent by friends and family).
4. Precut magazine pictures for the children to use.

Directions

1. Explain that a Joy Box is for keeping treasures that bring us joy. Show the children your Joy Box and the things in it. Explain why each item gives you joy.
2. Give each child a box.
3. Let the children use sequins, glitter, shells, magazine pictures, and glue to decorate their boxes.
4. Give each child the item you brought for his or her box. Let the children take their boxes home and encourage them to continue adding things to their Joy Boxes.

ACTIVITY: BAPTIZED IN GOD'S LOVE

Talk to the children about baptism. Explain how and when your church baptizes people. Discuss the meaning of baptism. During the next baptism, invite the children to come forward to watch a baptism up close. Ask parents to share the details of their children's baptisms. Prior to the program, encourage parents to bring pictures of their children being baptized.

Unscramble the word inside each baby present to reveal the message. Print the message on the lines at right.

UOY

SDAGESLN

JEROCIE

LLIW

DAN

TA

VHAE

Y
N
A
M

SIH

OYJ

LIWL

N
A
D

RIBTH

Chapter 19

BELIEVE IN JESUS

For God so loved the world that he gave his only Son, so that everyone who believes in him may not perish but may have eternal life.

—John 3:16

PROGRAM

GAME: HATCHING EGGS (See page 87.)

DISCUSSION

Discuss the meaning and importance of the Bible verse John 3:16 with the children. Explain the meaning of everlasting life.

BIBLE STORY: THE RESURRECTION STORY

(Matthew 28:1-15; Mark 16:1-8; Luke 24:1-12; John 20:1-18)
Tell the Resurrection story to the children. Explain that Jesus kept his promises to be raised from the dead, and that God loves us so much he sent Jesus to the world to save us from our sins. If we accept Christ as Lord and Savior of our lives, we too can have eternal life with God.

SONG: "YES, I BELIEVE!" RAP

Spoken Refrain:

Yes! I believe in Jesus! I believe! I believe in Jesus! OH YEAH!

Spoken Verse:

I believe that Jesus came to give us life! Eternal life!
That's what Jesus came to give! Eternal life! A life filled with love!

My soul will live on . . . forever . . . and ever . . . and ever! Yes! Forever!
(Repeat refrain)

SONG: "CHRIST THE LORD IS RISEN TODAY"

in *The Big Book of Hymns.*

ART: BANNERS OF BELIEF (See page 87.)

ACTIVITY: APOSTLES' CREED

Help the children learn and understand the Apostles' Creed. Ask your pastor to add the Apostles' Creed to worship during your study of John 3:16.

PROJECT: JESUS SAVES THE PEOPLE OF (CHURCH NAME) (See page 88.)

BULLETIN BOARD: ALLELUIA, CHRIST IS RISEN! (See pages 88-89.)

WORSHIP TIE-IN: YES, I BELIEVE!

Invite the children to share this rap during worship.

SOMETHING SPECIAL

Love One Another by Lauren Thompson
Learn about Jesus' final week on earth, his death and resurrection.

The Easter Story by Brian Wildsmith
The crucifixion, death, and resurrection of Jesus are retold using beautiful illustrations.

GAME: HATCHING EGGS

Materials

1 large empty Easter basket, 1 plastic colored Easter egg per child, colored markers, slips of paper, children's Easter cassette or CD and cassette or CD player, large poster board

Preparation

1. Print one word of the verse John 3:16 on each slip of paper. Put all the slips into one egg. Do this for each child.
2. Put the eggs into the basket.
3. Make the poster board with the Bible verse in large, easy-to-read letters. Keep it hidden until time for the children to read the verse.

Directions

1. Have the children sit in a circle and hand the basket to one of the children.
2. Play the music. Have the children pass the basket around the circle until the music stops. Have the child holding the basket choose an egg and leave the circle. Keep playing until each child has an egg. Tell the children not to open the eggs until the game is over.
3. Open the eggs and discover the strips of paper that have words written inside. Tell everyone to arrange the words in the proper order of the Bible verse.
4. Read the verse aloud together. Read it slowly, fast, and at normal speed.
5. Hold up the poster board and let the children read the verse together. Read it several times to allow the children to learn the words.

ART: BANNERS OF BELIEF

Materials

one 3-by-1-foot white heavy duty paper (or felt) banner per child, crayons and markers, sequins, stickers, foam shapes (examples: flowers, butterflies, suns, rainbows), letter stencils or dye cut machine, 1 envelope per child, two 14-inch wooden (or heavy cardboard) strips per child, yarn, glue, 1 copy of Bible verse John 3:16 for each child, construction paper

Preparation

1. Use stencils or a die cut machine and cut out one set of letters for each child that read I BELIEVE. Use a variety of colors.
2. Put each set of letters into an envelope.
3. Glue the wooden (or heavy cardboard) strips to the top and bottom of each banner and let dry.
4. Tie the yarn to the top strip of each banner.
5. Print a copy of the Bible verse for each child.

Directions

1. Give each child a banner and an envelope of letters.
2. Tell the children to glue their letters to the banner so I BELIEVE is readable.

3. Give each child a copy of the Bible verse to glue to his or her banner.
4. Let the children draw and color pictures on their banners using crayons and markers.
5. Let the children select foam shapes, stickers, and sequins to glue to their banners. Allow the banners to dry flat for the remainder of the program. Explain that the banners need to dry flat at home for 24 hours before hanging.

JESUS SAVES THE PEOPLE OF

(YOUR CHURCH NAME HERE)

Lisa Michaels

Anne Morley

Tommy Arnold

Katie Jones

James Patton

Ken Burton

PROJECT: JESUS SAVES THE PEOPLE OF (CHURCH NAME)

Materials

1 large color photograph of the outside of your church, white cardboard, crayons, markers, glitter, sequins, one 6-by-3-foot piece of plywood, white paint, and paintbrushes, glue or staple gun or heavy duty tacks, photos of church members, a basket of thin-tipped colorful felt pens (red, blue, green, purple), something with which to hang the board on the wall

Preparation

1. Paint the plywood white. Let dry completely.
2. Attach the photograph of the church to the center of the board.
3. Cut out letters from the white cardboard that read JESUS SAVES THE PEOPLE OF (CHURCH NAME).

Directions

1. Give each child one letter to decorate. Encourage the children to use crayons, markers, glitter, and sequins.
2. Attach the title to the board with glue, staple gun, or tacks.
3. Hang the board at eye level on a vacant wall in your building. Place the basket of thin-tipped colorful felt pens on a nearby table.

PROJECT: JESUS SAVES THE PEOPLE OF (NAME) ⇧

BULLETIN BOARD: ALLELUIA, CHRIST IS RISEN!

Materials

blue, green, white, yellow construction paper, red, yellow, pink, purple, orange, and dark green dry tempera paints, several sponges per paint color, 1 paintbrush, stapler or pushpins, white fiber fill, white cardboard, white glitter, glue, letter stencils or dye cut machine

4. Invite each church member to autograph the board. Ask church members to bring a photo to add alongside their autograph.
5. Keep the board displayed in a prominent place. It will attract lots of attention. Invite new members to autograph the board as they join the church.

Preparation

Directions
Give each child a sponge and let him or her sponge paint several flowers onto the stems.

1. Cover the bulletin board with blue paper. Cut the green paper to look like grass and put it along the bottom of the board.
2. Use white fiberfill to make clouds in the sky. Use glue to attach the clouds.
3. Make a sun from the yellow paper and attach it to the board.
4. Mix the tempera paints so they are quite thick.
5. Use green paint to make flower stems and leaves coming up from the grass and let dry.
6. Make a large cross from the white cardboard.
7. Glue glitter to the cross and let dry. Attach it to the center of the board.
8. Cut out letters with stencils or dye cut machine that read ALLELUIA, CHRIST IS RISEN!
9. Attach the title and the Bible verse John 3:16 to the board.

Alleluia! Christ Is Risen!

BULLETIN BOARD: ALLELUIA, CHRIST IS RISEN! ⇨

PUZZLE: WHAT?

Can you use the picture clues to discover the message? Print the correct words under each picture. Then read the message aloud.

4 God 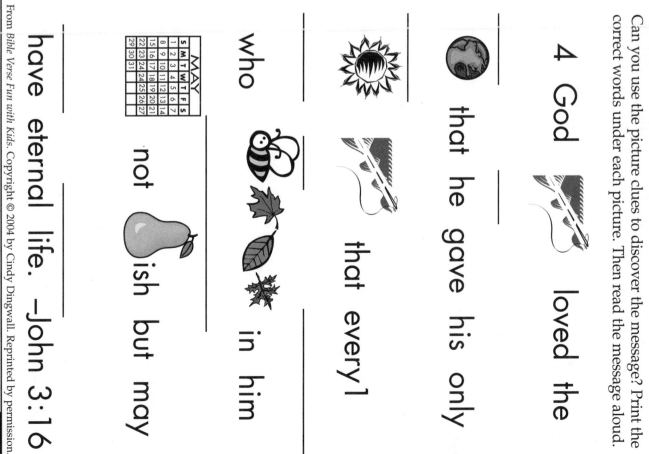 loved the ____ that he gave his only ____ that every1 ____ in him who ____ not ____ish but may have eternal life. –John 3:16

Chapter 20

REAPIN' REWARDS

The point is this: the one who sows sparingly will also reap sparingly, and the one who sows bountifully will also reap bountifully.
—2 Corinthians 9:6

PROGRAM

 ### GAME: MATCHING SEEDS (See page 91.)

BIBLE STORY: THE PARABLE OF THE SOWER (Matthew 13:1-23; Mark 4:1-20; Luke 8:4-15)

At least a week prior to sharing this lesson, plant different kinds of seeds: corn, lima bean, flowering seeds. Plant one lima bean seed on a piece of cotton and keep it watered, so the kids can see how the roots grow. Plant some seeds in sand, some in dirt (but do not water them) and some in rich soil that is kept properly watered. Have some unplanted seeds to show as well.

As you share this parable with the children, show the different plants as the story indicates. Discuss the story. Talk about what happened to the seeds you planted: What happened to the seeds planted in the sand? What happened to the seeds planted in the soil that was not watered? What happened to the seeds planted in the rich soil and given plenty of water? Talk about the roots of the seed. Why are roots necessary? Explain that like a plant needs roots to get water and nutrients from the soil, our beliefs need to be rooted in the Lord to get spiritual nourishment.

Explain that our lives are very much like these plants, and that we also need water and nutrition to grow strong and healthy. Talk about what happens when we fill our minds and hearts with God's Word and love. Tell the children we can sow God's seeds of love and goodness wherever we go. Talk about the many ways we can do this.

SOMETHING SPECIAL

The Surprise Garden
by Zoe Hall
    The kids were surprised at the wonderful garden they grew.

Parables: Stories Jesus Told
by Mary Hoffman
    This book includes the Parable of the Sower.

SONG: "ALL AROUND THE WORLD"
("Pop Goes the Weasel")

All around the world,
God's plantin' seeds of love.
God wants us all to go around,
And share these seeds of love!
Share that love with everyone,
Everyone we meet!
Share that love with everyone,
Everyone you meet!

 ### ART: FLOWER VASES (See page 91.)

 ### PROJECT: GARDEN OF FAITH (See pages 91-92.)

BULLETIN BOARD: A GARDEN OF GOD'S FOLLOWERS (See page 92.)

WORSHIP TIE-IN: ALL AROUND THE WORLD

Invite the children to sing this song (page 90) during congregational worship. Let kids toss out confetti hearts at the end of the song.

GAME: MATCHING SEEDS

Materials

2 pictures of 23 different seeds, black felt marker, 46 index cards, glue or glue sticks

Preparation

1. Glue one picture of each seed to an index card. You should have two identical cards for each seed. Divide these into duplicate sets. Set one set of seed cards aside.
2. On the other set of cards, print one word of the Bible verse 2 Corinthians 9:6 on the back of each card. Hide these cards in different places around your room.

Directions

1. Give each child one seed card. Tell the children to find the seed card that matches the one they have.
2. After all of the matching cards have been found, put the Bible verse in the correct order.

HINTS

If you have a large group, divide the children into teams and let them search for the matching card as a team. With a smaller group, let some or all of the children look for more than one card.

ART: FLOWER VASES

Materials

1 clear glass flower vase per child, glass enamel paints in a variety of bright colors, several paintbrushes per paint color

Directions

1. Give each child a glass vase. Warn the children to be careful with the glass.
2. Use the paints to create designs on the vases and let dry.

PROJECT: GARDEN OF FAITH

Materials

outdoor planting area with easily accessible hose and water, topsoil, trowels, seeds or annual flowers, appropriate fertilizer

Preparation

1. Decide whether to plant a vegetable or flower garden and gather the appropriate seeds or plants.
2. Prepare the area for planting by removing debris and weeds.
3. Remind the kids to wear old clothing that can get dirty.

Directions

1. Talk about how we prepare the soil for accepting seeds. Discuss the kind of garden you will plant, nurture, and grow.

2. Help the children spread the topsoil. Mix in the fertilizer.
3. Sow the seeds for vegetables or plant the annual flowers.
4. Weed and water the garden on a regular basis. Have the children visit their garden each week.
5. If you grow vegetables, "sell" them to the congregation and use the money for your Sunday school program.
6. If growing flowers, consider using them on the altar during Sunday worship, taking them to homebound or hospitalized church members, or letting the children take them home and create a flower arrangement in their flower vases.

HINT

Keep track of where you plant each kind of seed.

BULLETIN BOARD: A GARDEN OF GOD'S FOLLOWERS

Materials

blue, green, and yellow construction paper, white batting, stapler or pushpins, green crepe paper, dry tempera paints, several flower-shaped sponges per paint color, glue, scissors, instant camera and film, letter stencils or dye cut machine

Preparation

1. Attach the blue paper to the board to make the sky. Make and attach a sun from yellow paper. Glue the white batting to the board to make clouds.
2. Put the green paper on the board to make the grass. Use scissors to cut fringe, so it has a three-dimensional grassy effect.
3. Cut and fold the green crepe paper to make flower stems and leaves. Attach these to the board with pushpins or staples.
4. Cut out the title A GARDEN OF GOD'S FOLLOWERS using stencils or dye cut machine.
5. Attach the title using pushpins or staples.
6. Mix the tempera paints so they are thick.

Directions

1. Take photos of the kids throughout the program. Let the kids have fun posing for these. Take individual and group shots.
2. Have the children take turns sponge painting flowers onto the bulletin board. Let the paint dry.
3. Use pushpins to attach the pictures to the flower garden, so the photos are among the flowers.

BULLETIN BOARD: A GARDEN OF GOD'S FOLLOWERS

PUZZLE: SOWING GOD'S LOVE

Begin at the arrow and color the petals marked P pink. Then color the rest of the petals yellow. Print the words colored pink first, starting at the arrow and going clockwise. Then print the words colored yellow. What's the message?

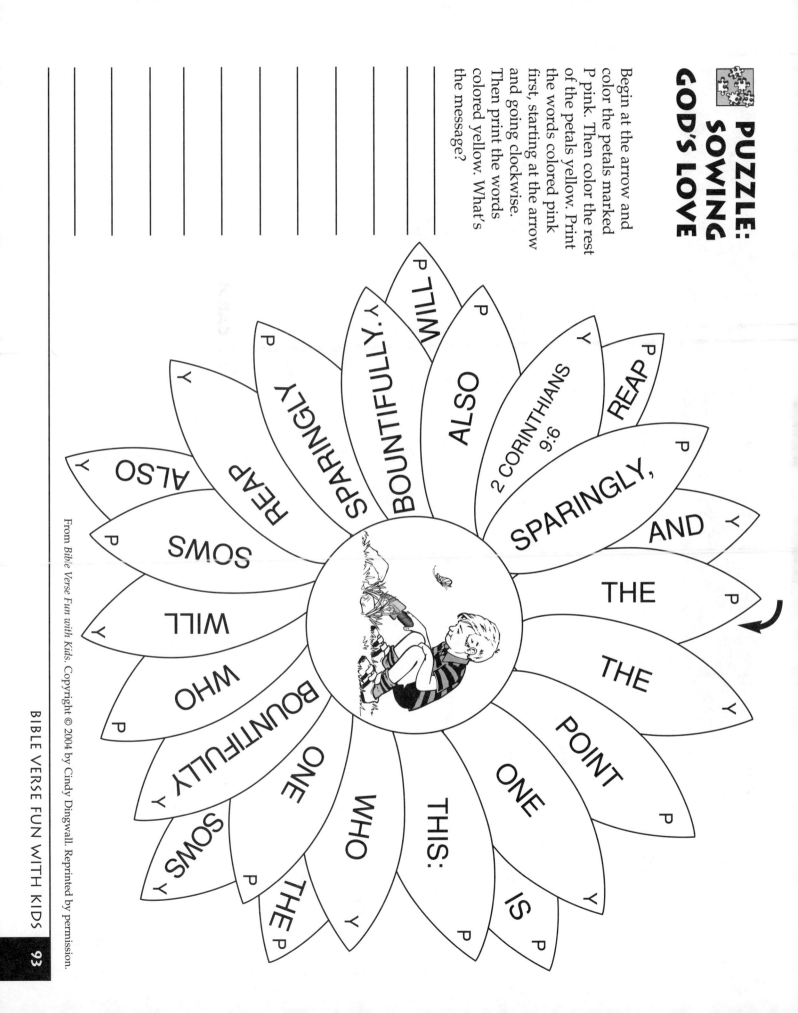

2 CORINTHIANS 9:6

REAP

SPARINGLY,

AND

THE

THE

POINT

ONE

IS

P

THIS:

WHO

THE

SOWS

BOUNTIFULLY

WHO

WILL

SOWS

ALSO

REAP

SPARINGLY

BOUNTIFULLY.

WILL

ALSO

Chapter 21

THE ARMOR OF GOD

Put on the full armor of God so that you can take your stand against the devil's schemes.

—Ephesians 6:11 NIV

PROGRAM

GAME: CAN'T STOP ME! (See page 95.)

BIBLE STORY: THE FULL ARMOR OF GOD

(Ephesians 6:10-18)
Share this story with the children.

DISCUSSION

Talk about the armor biblical soldiers wore when they went into battle. Explain how we, like soldiers going into battle, must arm ourselves against temptation. Discuss how present day soldiers dress for battle and how they defend themselves. Ask the children what temptations they face. Encourage the children to share how they handle temptations, conflicts, and disagreements.

ACTIVITY: STRENGTHENED BY GOD
(See page 95.)

SONG: "ONWARD, CHRISTIAN SOLDIERS"
in *The Big Book of Hymns.*

ART: A SHIELD OF WISDOM (See page 96.)

PROJECT: SUPPORT OUR TROOPS (See pages 96-97.)

BULLETIN BOARD: PROTECTED BY GOD (See page 97.)

WORSHIP TIE-IN: MY DUTY TO MY COUNTRY

Ask members of your congregation who have served in the armed services to share their experiences with the children. Invite guests to tell why they decided to enter the armed services and to explain the importance of the military.

SOMETHING SPECIAL

If You Were There: Biblical Times
by Antony Mason
This book includes excellent drawings and information about the armor warriors wore in biblical times.

GAME: CAN'T STOP ME!

Ephesians 6:11 NIV

Materials

cardstock paper, laminating film and machine or clear contact paper, black marker, yarn, hole punch, bucket, 1 volunteer to portray the devil

Preparation

1. Cut out 18 shields from cardstock.
2. Print one word from the Bible verse Ephesians 6:11 on each shield. Laminate or cover each shield with clear contact paper.
3. Cut eighteen 36-inch strands of yarn.
4. Punch a hole in the top of each shield and string with yarn. Tie the ends of the yarn to make a big loop.
5. Place the shields in the bucket.

Directions

1. Invite each child to choose a shield from the bucket. Instruct the children to hang the shields around their necks.
2. Let the children read the words on the shields in random order. Ask the kids what they can do so that the words make sense. If needed, suggest they work together to arrange themselves in the correct order to discover the Bible verse.
3. As the children arrange themselves in the proper order, the volunteer portraying the devil will try to stop them. After awhile, the devil gives up and says, "I guess you are much stronger than I am." The devil leaves.
4. Once the kids have arranged themselves in the correct order, form a circle. Read the verse together.

ACTIVITY: STRENGTHENED BY GOD

Materials

silver cardboard, 18-inch lengths of yarn, football helmet, hole punch, black marker, laminating film and machine or clear contact paper

Preparation

1. Cut a breastplate from shiny silver cardboard.
2. Use black marker to print the Bible verse Ephesians 6:11 on the breastplate.
3. Laminate or cover it with clear contact paper. Punch holes in the top and attach the yarn, making a loop to go over the children's necks.
4. Make several small shields. Use black marker to print a situation on each shield. (Examples: (1) *Your best friend is having trouble in math, wants to copy your homework, and threatens to stop being your friend if you refuse.* (2) *Your friend sees something at the store, doesn't have enough money, and wants to steal it while you distract the salesperson.* (3) *You see some bullies being mean to a new kid but are afraid you will be called a tattletale if you tell or that they may gang up on you.*)
5. Laminate or cover the shields with clear contact paper.

Directions

1. Put the shields into a football helmet. Let each child wear the breastplate as he or she selects a shield.
2. Have each child read his or her shield. Ask: What are you tempted to do? What does God want you to do? What would you really do?

ART: A SHIELD OF WISDOM

Materials

1 wooden shield per child (pattern on this page), 1 copy of the Bible verse Ephesians 6:11 per child, decoupage glue, dark brown wood stain, paintbrush, glue, picture hanging hooks, clear contact paper, glitter, sequins, other decorations

Preparation

1. Reduce the size of the shield pattern and type the Bible verse so that it will fit inside. Cut out the paper shields and cover with contact paper.

2. Stain the wooden shields and let dry. Attach a picture hook to the back of each shield.

Directions

1. Give each child a shield and have him or her glue the Bible verse to it.

2. Use the glitter and sequins to decorate the shields and let dry.

PROJECT: SUPPORT OUR TROOPS

Talk about how our military help keep us safe from harm. Ask if any child has relatives in the armed forces now or had in the past. Invite current or past members of the military in your church to visit (in uniform, if possible) to talk about their work.

Contact a nearby military installation to obtain the addresses of military personnel stationed in the United States or overseas. Have the children make cards and drawings, or write letters thanking them for their service to our country. Send these to the individuals on

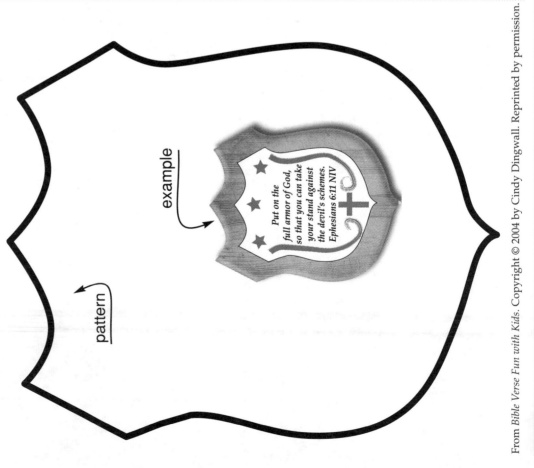

pattern

example

Put on the full armor of God, so that you can take your stand against the devil's schemes. Ephesians 6:11 NIV

your list, making sure to include a return address. Explain that sometimes security measures prevent soldiers from respond-ing. If you do get a response, share it with the children.

IDEA

If national security prevents you from sending mail to U.S. troops stationed overseas, send your creations to a nearby veteran's hospital or send a message on www.operationdear abby.net. Children may become a part of the Presidential Prayer Team at www.presidentialprayerteam.org.

3. Attach the shields to the bulletin board.

protection to help them from temptation. Let the children print these thoughts on the shields.

BULLETIN BOARD: PROTECTED BY GOD

Materials

black construction paper for background, letter stencils or dye cut machine, silver cardboard, colored construction paper, bright colored markers, silver paper

Preparation

1. Cover the board with the black construction paper.
2. Cut out letters for the title PROTECTED BY GOD from sil-ver paper. Attach to the board.
3. Cut a large shield from silver cardboard. Print the Bible verse Ephesians 6:11 on the shield.
4. Attach the large shield with the verse to the center of the board.
5. Make one colored construction paper shield per child.

Directions

1. Give each child a colored shield and a marker.
2. Ask the children to think about ways they can use God's

BULLETIN BOARD: PROTECTED BY GOD ➪

PROTECTED BY GOD

Put on the full armor of God, so that you can take your stand against the devil's schemes. Ephesians 6:11 NIV

PUZZLE: WHAT SHOULD I WEAR?

Use a yellow marker or crayon to color each word as you find it in the puzzle. The left-over words answer the question, "What should I wear?"

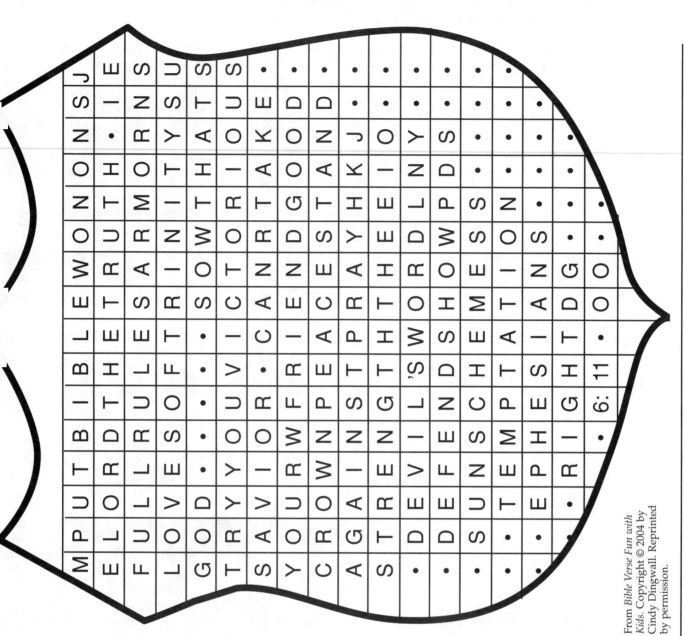

Temptation	Trinity
	Bible
Show	Won
	Kind
Victorious	Crown
	Truth
Good	Sun
	Joys
Defend	Friend
	Loves
Rules	Own
	Sins
Savior	Peace
	Jesus
Lord	Strength
	Try
Right	Helps
	Pray
Me	Go
	Do

Word (appears twice!) _____

Print the message here: _____

_____

_____

From *Bible Verse Fun with Kids*. Copyright © 2004 by Cindy Dingwall. Reprinted by permission.

RACE FOR THE LORD

I press on toward the goal for the prize of the heavenly call of God in Christ Jesus.

—Philippians 3:14

PROGRAM

GAME: EGG-CITING RELAY (See page 100.)

BIBLE STORY: RACIN' TOWARD GOD
(Philippians 3:12-16)
Share this story with the children.

SOMETHING SPECIAL

The Tortoise and the Hare by Aesop (illustrated by Janet Stevens or Brian Wildsmith)

Present this as a puppet show. Ask two junior or senior high students to act out the story with a turtle puppet and a rabbit puppet. You can be the narrator. Practice with your helpers prior to the program.

DISCUSSION

Explain what goal setting is. Doing better in math, playing a musical instrument, a clean room are all goals. How do we go about achieving our goals? Tell the children that rather than complain about what we have to do to attain our goals, it is better to concentrate on doing

what we need to do to achieve our goals. Remind the children that God is rooting for us to do our best. We can pray to God, who will help us as we strive to achieve our goals.

SONG: "I'M GONNA KEEP ON A-TRYIN'"
("Down by the Riverside")

I'm gonna keep on a-tryin'
To do the best I can
To do the best I can
To do the best I can
I'm gonna keep on a-tryin'
To do the best I can
And the good Lord will always help me!

(Encourage kids to think of verses: "I'm gonna learn how to do that math, and do the best I can," "I'm gonna learn how to swim real good, and do the best I can," "I'm gonna be a nice kid, and do the best I can.")

ART: RACING SHOES (See pages 100-101.)

PROJECT: MOVIN' FOR THE LORD (See page 101.)

BULLETIN BOARD: RUNNING TOWARD JESUS (See page 103.)

WORSHIP TIE-IN: THE TORTOISE AND THE HARE

Ask your church's youth group to present this puppet show during congregational worship. Divide the children into two groups. One will cheer on the tortoise and the other will cheer on the hare.

GAME: EGG-CITING RELAY

Materials

1 large basket per team, 18 colored plastic eggs per team, masking tape, colored markers, eighteen 1-by-4-inch strips of paper per team, children's Christian cassette or CD and cassette or CD player

Preparation

(*Note: Do the following for each team of kids.*)

1. Print one word of the verse Philippians 3:14 on each strip of paper.
2. Put one strip into each egg. Put the eggs into the basket.
3. Designate an area to run the relay. Place the baskets at the end of the running lane.
4. Mark the starting line with a piece of masking tape along the floor. Have the children stand behind this line while waiting their turn.
5. Gather prizes for the teams, for example, candy bars for the members of the winning team and small chocolates for the other teams.

Directions

1. Divide the group into teams and have each group form a single

file line behind the masking tape line. Play music.
2. Explain that each person will run to the basket, pick up an egg, and bring it back. When they return to the masking tape line, it is the next member's turn.
3. After the team picks up all the eggs, the team sits down, opens the eggs, and takes out the paper inside. Now the team will put the verse in the correct order. See which team can discover the verse first.
4. Distribute prizes to the children.

ART: RACING SHOES

Materials

1 pair of gym shoes per child, fabric paints, glitter, sequins, other decorations, fabric glue, 1 pair of colorful long shoelaces per child

Preparation

Ask each person to bring a pair of inexpensive, new, plain white canvas gym shoes.

Directions

1. Let each child use the fabric paints, glitter, sequins to decorate his or her shoes.

IDEA

Have the members of a team choose different ways of getting to the basket such as hop, skip, jump, or crawl rather than run to get to the basket. For example, the first person could hop, the second could skip, the third might crawl.

HINT

You may need to have some kids run the relay more than one time.

2. Give each child a pair of shoelaces to add to his or her shoes. Encourage the children to wear their racing shoes to Sunday school each week.

PROJECT: MOVIN' FOR THE LORD

Materials

jump ropes, large rubber balls, one volunteer counter per child, gym or other open area

Preparation

1. Enlist junior and senior high students or adults to be counters.
2. Provide pledge sheets (page 102) for the children and ask them to find 5 to 10 pledgers. Have the children seek pledges from members of the congregation, neighbors, friends, and family members. Pledges can begin at a penny a jump, bounce, or lap. Pledge amounts may go as high as the pledger chooses, or consider setting a specific amount such as $5.00 per pledge.
3. Reserve a gymnasium or other open area where the children can be active.

Directions

1. Let each child decide how he or she wants to move, for example, jump rope, toss balls against walls or to one another, bounce balls, run laps, walk laps, jumping, or other activity.
2. Have the children bring their pledge sheets with them on Movin' for the Lord Day.

3. Assign each child a volunteer who counts the number of jumps, hops, ball bounces, and so on the child does. The counter will write the total on each child's pledge sheet. Set a time limit of 5 to 15 minutes that each person has to do their moves.
4. Provide a lunch of hot dogs, chips, cookies, and juice for all participants.
5. Have the children collect the money they earned from their pledgers.
6. Use the money raised to purchase something special for your Sunday school program.

MOVIN'
FOR THE LORD PLEDGE SHEET

Your Name: _____

(First)   (Last)

Your Activity:

☐ jump rope   ☐ jump up and down   ☐ run laps   ☐ walk laps   ☐ bounce ball

PLEDGER'S NAME	ADDRESS	PHONE	AMOUNT

Movin' Total: _____

TOTAL AMOUNT OF MONEY RAISED: _____

BULLETIN BOARD: RUNNING TOWARD JESUS

Materials

one 10-inch wide piece of white butcher paper (about 10 feet long), a long wall, large picture of Jesus standing, glue, heavy duty tape, letter stencils or dye cut machine, colored markers, colored tempera paints, paintbrushes, kids' feet (with or without shoes), paper towels, water, disposable pie tins, newspapers, volunteer to portray Jesus, 1 cookie per child

Preparation

1. Mix the tempera paints so they are thick. Put one color of paint into each pie tin.
2. Lay newspapers in a wide area, preferably on a hard floor, to catch any paint drips.
3. Lay the white butcher paper on top of the newspapers.

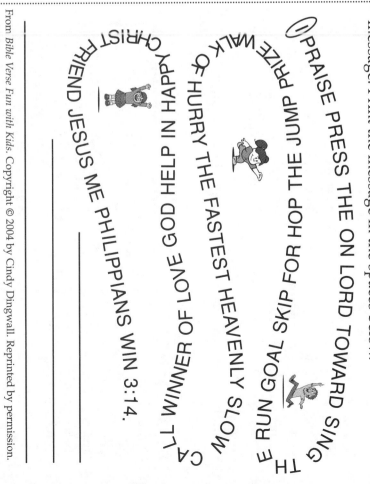

Directions

1. Ask the volunteer portraying Jesus to greet the children and give them cookies.
2. Let the children choose a paint color. One at a time, paint the bottom of each child's feet. Let the child walk across the paper toward Jesus. Afterwards, wash his or her feet with water and wipe dry with paper towels.
3. Let the paper dry after each child has had a chance to walk across it.
4. When the paper is dry, use colored markers to autograph it.
5. Hang the butcher paper on the wall with heavy duty tape. Tape the large picture of Jesus at the end of the mural. Add the title RUNNING TOWARD JESUS above the mural.

BULLETIN BOARD: RUNNING TOWARD JESUS

RUNNING TOWARD JESUS!!! ⇨

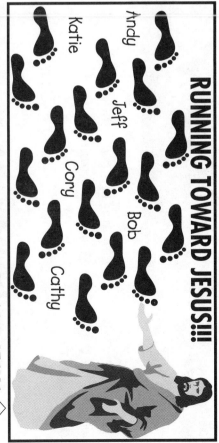

Andy

Katie

Jeff

Cory

Bob

Cathy

PUZZLE: RUNNING THE RACE

Circle every other word on the path to Jesus to discover the message. Print the message in the spaces below.

PRAISE PRESS THE ON LORD TOWARD SING THE RUN GOAL SKIP FOR HOP HOP THE JUMP PRIZE WALK OF HURRY THE FASTEST HEAVENLY SLOW CALL WINNER OF LOVE GOD HELP IN HAPPY CHRIST FRIEND JESUS ME PHILIPPIANS WIN 3:14.

_____

_____

Chapter 23

RANDOM ACTS OF KINDNESS

*As God's chosen ones, holy and beloved, clothe your-
selves with compassion, kindness, humility, meekness,
and patience.*

—Colossians 3:12

PROGRAM

GAME: PASS THE HAT (See page 105.)

DISCUSSION

Talk about how we put on clothes each day. Talk about the
different kinds of clothes we wear: play clothes, school
clothes, dress up clothes, sports team clothes. Talk about why
we wear clothes. Read the Bible verse Colossians 3:12. Relate
wearing clothes to the words in the Bible verse. Ask: What
does God want us to clothe our souls in? Tell the children we
are going to focus on clothing ourselves in kindness. Ask:
What does kindness mean? How do we show kindness?

BIBLE STORY

Choose a favorite
Bible story that high-
lights Jesus showing
kindness to others.
Share it with the chil-
dren. Tell them why
it is your favorite
story about Jesus.

Ask the children to tell you about their favorite stories about
Jesus showing kindness.

ART: "KIND HANDS" SHIRTS (See pages
105-106.)

PROJECT: SPREADING THE KINDNESS

Give each child a packet of seeds and a note that says,
"I am giving you this pack of seeds as an act of kindness.
Please do something kind for someone else." Encourage each
child to anonymously give the seeds and note to a neighbor.

SONG: "OH, LET'S BE KIND!" (*"When the Saints Go
Marching In"*)

Oh, let's be kind! (clap, clap, clap, clap)
Oh, let's be kind! (clap, clap, clap, clap)
Oh, let's be kind to one another!
Let's show the world that God is love!
Oh, let's be kind to one another! (clap, clap, clap, clap)

Let's help a friend! (stamp, stamp, stamp, stamp)
Let's help a friend! (stamp, stamp, stamp, stamp)
Oh, let's be kind to one another!
Let's show the world that God is love!
Oh, let's be kind to one another! (stamp, stamp, stamp,
stamp)

Let the kids think of additional verses and movements.

SOMETHING SPECIAL

Glenna's Seeds by Nancy Edwards
When Glenna shared a packet of
seeds with a neighbor, she started
a whole bunch of kind acts among
the neighbors in her world.

BULLETIN BOARD: RANDOM ACTS OF KINDNESS (See page 106.)

WORSHIP TIE-IN: "OH, LET'S BE KIND!"

Invite the kids to sing the song on the previous page for congregational worship.

GAME: PASS THE HAT

Materials

1 large hat, construction paper, colored felt markers, Christian children's cassette or CD and cassette or CD player

Preparation

1. Using the pattern on this page, cut out 16 large construction paper hats.
2. Print one word of the verse Colossians 3:12 on each construction paper hat.
3. Put construction paper hats into the large hat.

Directions

1. Have the children sit in a circle.
2. Give one of the children the large hat.
3. Play the music. Let the children pass the hat around the circle while it plays.
4. Stop the music. The child holding the hat pulls a construction paper hat out of the large hat and leaves the circle. Keep playing until each child has a construction paper hat.
5. Have the children figure out how to put themselves in the correct order so they can read the verse.
6. Now, have the children make a circle and hold their paper hats so everyone can see them. Read the verse out loud together.

pattern

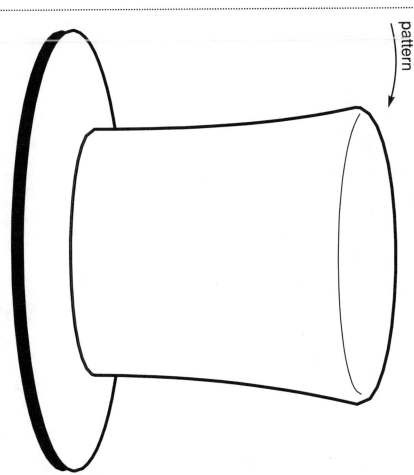

From *Bible Verse Fun with Kids.* Copyright © 2004 by Cindy Dingwall. Reprinted by permission.

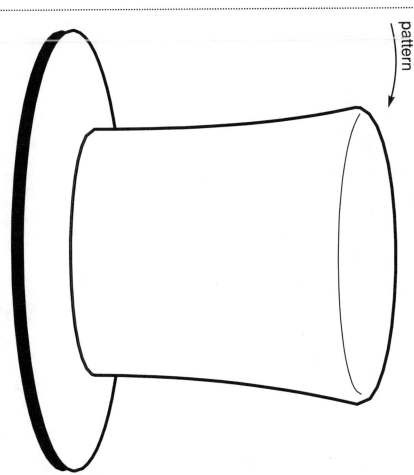

ART: "KIND HANDS" SHIRTS

Materials

1 white or pastel colored T-shirt per child, fabric crayons, fabric paints, glitter, glue, cardboard, permanent marker

Preparation

1. Contact each child's parent or guardian and request that his or her child bring a clean, new, white or pastel-colored

T-shirt that fits. Ask parents to wash the shirt without fabric softener. Gather these at least one week before the program. Label each shirt with the child's name.

2. Cut cardboard to fit inside each shirt. This will keep the paint from gluing the front of the shirt to the back.

3. Use fabric crayons and paints to print the Bible verse Colossians 3:12 on the front of each child's shirt. Let these dry thoroughly.

Directions

1. Give each child his or her shirt.

2. Let each child paint one hand with fabric paint and make one handprint on all of the shirts. When finished, the children should have a shirt that sports a handprint from each classmate.

3. Let dry before wearing. Encourage children to wear their "kind hands" shirts to church activities.

BULLETIN BOARD: RANDOM ACTS OF KINDNESS

Materials

Christian-themed wrapping paper, handprint for each child, colored thin felt markers, bright construction paper, stapler or pushpins, letter stencils or dye cut machine

Preparation

1. Cover the bulletin board with the wrapping paper.

2. Create the title RANDOM ACTS OF KINDNESS from stencils or dye cuts.

Attach it to the board using staples or pushpins.

3. Create a handprint pattern by tracing a hand. Make 5 to 10 handprints per child from colored construction paper.

Directions

1. Give each child a paper handprint. Encourage children to think of kind things they can do. Have each child print his or her kindness on the paper hand. Use staples or pushpins to attach each paper hand to the board.

2. Give each child a package of 5 to 10 paper hands to take home. Encourage them to practice "random acts of kindness" all week long. Tell them to write each random act of kindness on a hand. Have the children bring back the hands the following week and tell about the random acts of kindness they did during the week. Add these hands to the board.

IDEA

Involve the entire congregation of your church in your "random acts of kindness" marathon. Let each member of the congregation use paper hands to list their random acts of kindness. See how many random acts of kindness everyone can perform this week. Once started, keep it going! List the random acts of kindnesses in your church newsletter and on your church Web site.

HINT

Send a note home to parents explaining the random acts of kindness. Offer ways that parents can help their children perform random acts of kindness.

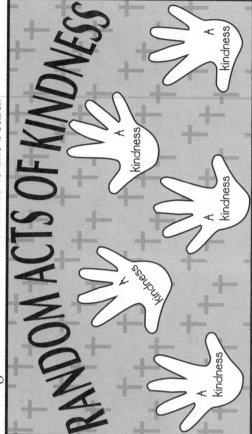

RANDOM ACTS OF KINDNESS

PUZZLE: LET'S DO IT!

Cross out words that begin with the letter Z.
Cross out words that are COLORS.
Cross out words that are BODY PARTS.
Cross out words that end with the letter K.
Cross out the word for the number 2.
Cross out words that are HOLIDAYS.
Cross out words that rhyme with DOG.

FROG AS ZEBRAS TOES GOD'S HEAD CHOSEN ONES STARK HOLY HANDS NOSE AND DARK EYES BELOVED MARK

CHRISTMAS CLOTHE ZAP THANKSGIVING YOURSELVES TWO WITH ZIPPERS RED COMPASSION GREEN KINDNESS

BLUE FEET HUMILITY TWO PURPLE MEEKNESS ZONE HOG AND ORANGE PATIENCE EASTER FOG.

Print the verse in the spaces below.

_____

_____

_____

_____

_____.

Colossians 3:12

From *Bible Verse Fun with Kids*.
Copyright © 2004 by Cindy Dingwall.
Reprinted by permission.

Chapter 24

ANCHORS AWEIGH!

We have this hope as an anchor for the soul, firm and secure.

—Hebrews 6:19 NIV

PROGRAM

GAME: ANCHORED BY JESUS (See page 109.)

BIBLE STORY: PAUL SAILS FOR ROME

(Acts 27)

Tell this story to the children. Bring Bible storybooks that show the type of ship Paul sailed on. Explain that the cargo ships that sailed the Mediterranean Sea could carry 200-300 people as well as cargo. These ships were very rustic, unlike the modern ships we cruise on today. Show the children a map that depicts the voyage; Bibles are a good source of this information.

DISCUSSION

Emphasize how Paul and those sailing with him used the anchors to not only slow down the ship during a storm, but also to secure the ship while in port. Talk about how the words, teachings, and love of Jesus are anchors for our lives. Ask how God's words and love can anchor us. Discuss how Paul and those traveling with him were very frightened during the storm and about how God's love was the anchor that gave them courage.

SONG: "THE ANCHOR OF GOD" (*"When Johnny Comes Marching Home"*)

God is the anchor for our soul, Oh yeah, Oh yeah,
God's love is firm and secure for all, Oh yeah, Oh yeah,
God gives us strength to get through tough things,
God gives us such love and many blessings,
So let's all hold firm to God's anchor of love for us!

ART: ANCHORED TO JESUS (See page 110.)

PROJECT: ANCHORS FOR ALL

Follow the instructions for the art project on page 110. Make an anchor for each staff member of your congregation. Let the children present these to each staff member during congregational worship.

IDEA

Bring anchors with chains for the children to see and touch. Let them feel how sturdy and heavy the anchors are. If possible, firmly plant anchors in the dirt outside, and let the children try to pull them out of the ground.

SOMETHING SPECIAL

Sailing to the Sea
by Mary-Claire Helldofer
What an exciting sailboat journey!

Moonlight on the River
by Deborah Kovacs
One night, two boys snuck out for an adventure-filled sail.

BULLETIN BOARD: JESUS IS OUR ANCHOR (See page 110.)

WORSHIP TIE-IN: THE ANCHOR OF GOD

Invite the kids to sing this song (page 108) for congregational worship. If possible, get sailor hats for the kids to wear. Put a large anchor on the altar where they will stand.

GAME: ANCHORED BY JESUS

Materials

15 wooden anchors or plywood, black permanent marker, several buckets, sand, 1 nail, fifteen 10-inch strands of leather

Preparation

1. Purchase or make wooden anchors from pattern on this page. Ask a handy person to cut these from plywood, if necessary.

2. Use the permanent marker to print one word of the Bible verse on each anchor. Print *Hebrews* on one anchor and *6:19* on another anchor.

3. Use the nail to poke a hole in the top of each anchor.

4. Thread one strand of leather through each anchor.

5. Fill several buckets with sand. Bury each anchor in the sand.

HINT

With smaller groups, some or all children can pull out more than one anchor. With large groups, have the children work in teams. Make one set of anchors and buckets per team. See which team of "sailors" can pull out their anchors and decipher the verse first.

Directions

1. Let each child pull an anchor out of the sand.

2. Have the children arrange themselves in the correct order to reveal the verse.

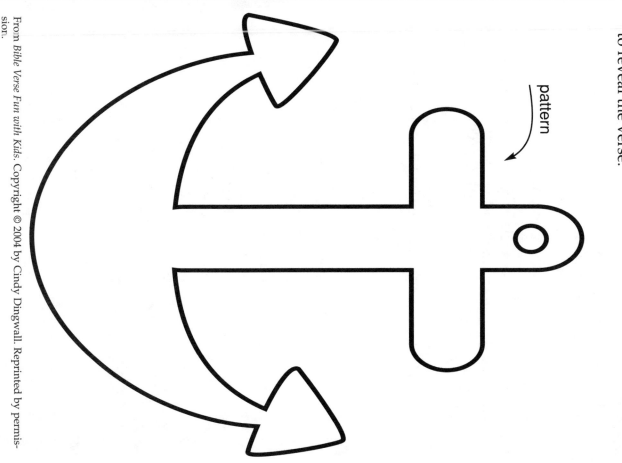

pattern

ART: ANCHORED TO JESUS

Materials

1 wooden anchor per child or plywood, one 12-inch strand of leather per child, 1 unlined index card per child, permanent black markers, hole punch, nail, crayons

Preparation

1. Purchase precut wooden anchors or cut them from plywood using the pattern on page 109.
2. Use a permanent marker to print HEBREWS 6:19 on the front of each anchor. Print ANCHORED TO JESUS along the bottom of the back of each anchor.
3. Use a nail to poke a hole through the top of each anchor.
4. Print the Bible verse Hebrews 6:19 on each index card. Punch a hole in the top of each card.

Directions

1. Give each child an anchor and a permanent black marker to print his or her name on the back of each anchor.
2. Use crayons to color the anchors.
3. Distribute the index cards with the verse.
4. String a piece of leather through the top of the anchor. Thread the card on the leather string. The children can hang the anchors at home.

BULLETIN BOARD: JESUS IS OUR ANCHOR

Materials

medium blue paper, darker blue paper, blue food wrap, one 6-by-1-inch strip of light gray paper per child, large colored picture of Jesus, silver cardboard, stapler or pushpins, white

construction paper, letter stencils or dye cut machine, brown construction paper

Preparation

1. Attach the medium blue paper for the sky. Cut the darker blue paper to look like waves and attach it to the bottom of the bulletin board.
2. Use the stencils or dye cut machine to create the title JESUS IS OUR ANCHOR and attach it to the board.
3. Make a large boat from brown construction paper. Attach the boat to the board. Put Jesus in the boat.
4. Enlarge the pattern on page 109 for the anchor. Trace it onto silver cardboard.

Directions

1. Give the children a gray paper strip and have them print their name.
2. Staple a paper chain with the strips, making sure that the children's names show.
3. Tape the anchor to the end of the paper chain.
4. Attach the chain to the bulletin board so that Jesus is holding the unanchored end of the chain. Drape the chain over the side of the boat and attach the anchor to the chain with the anchor in the water.
5. Cover the water, the end of the chain, the anchor, and the bottom of the boat with blue food wrap to imitate water.

JESUS IS OUR ANCHOR

PUZZLE: WHAT DO WE HAVE?

Sailors use coordinates to help them navigate their ships. Use the coordinates below to help you decode the message. Print it below.

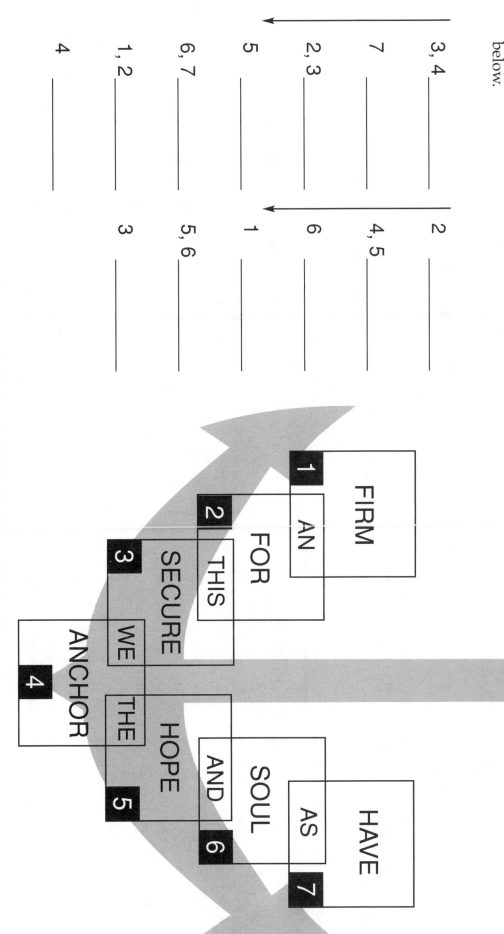

3, 4 _____ 2 _____

7 _____

2, 3 _____ 4, 5 _____ 6 _____

5 _____ 1 _____

6, 7 _____ 5, 6 _____

1, 2 _____ 3 _____

4 _____

Chapter 25

SHARING GOD'S LOVE

Do not neglect to do good and to share what you have, for such sacrifices are pleasing to God.

—Hebrews 13:16

PROGRAM

GAME: SHARE IT! (See page 113.)

BIBLE STORY: A WIDOW GIVES ALL SHE HAS (Mark 12:41-44)
Tell this story to the children.

DISCUSSION
Discuss the story of the widow and relate it to our lives today. Why does God want us to share? How does sharing help others? What would happen if no one ever shared anything? Tie this story in with what happened when you broke the piñata in the "Share It!" game.

SONG: "PASS IT ON"
by Kurt Kaiser in *The Big Book of Contemporary Christian Favorites*

ART: SHARING BOXES (See page 113.)

PROJECT: BASKETS TO SHARE
(See page 114.)

BULLETIN BOARD: SHARING GOD'S LOVE (See pages 114-115.)

WORSHIP TIE-IN: COME ON, SHARE . . . PLEASE

Prepare two big baskets of individually-wrapped candies. Place one basket on your lap. Keep the other basket out of sight. Invite the kids to join you at the altar. Start opening and eating the candies. When the children ask you to share, tell them you are going to eat them all yourself. Ask the children if they want some candy. Of course they do! Respond with, "Well, I'm not going to eat them all myself!" Respond to their reaction by asking why it is better for you to share rather than eat all the candy yourself. Discuss why God wants us to share. Give each child a piece of candy. Pull out the other baskets of candy and invite the children to give the remaining pieces to people in the congregation.

SOMETHING SPECIAL

The Best Night Out with Dad by Lisa McCourt
Danny is faced with the decision of whether or not to share his circus tickets with a less fortunate friend.

Rosie and the Poor Rabbits by Maryann MacDonald
Rosie doesn't want to share her things.

GAME: SHARE IT!

Materials

one piñata, 20 index cards, felt pens, small inexpensive toys and individually wrapped candies, stick for hitting piñata, rope for hanging the piñata, hook to hang piñata on

Preparation

1. Use the felt pens to print one word of the Bible verse Hebrews 13:16 on each index card.
2. Place the index cards, toys, and candy inside the piñata and seal it.
3. Use the rope to hang the piñata on the hook.

Directions

1. Have the kids sit in a circle on the floor under the piñata. Allow plenty of room.
2. Take turns hitting the piñata with the stick.
3. When the piñata breaks, let the children grab what they can.
4. See if the children notice that they also have index cards with words written on them. Ask: Do you think these cards have a message for us? Let's see if we can figure out what the message is.
5. After discovering the message, see if they can apply it to their newfound goodies. Ask: What are we going to do about the candy and toys here? Hopefully, the children will decide on their own to share it, but if not, gently suggest this.

ART: SHARING BOXES

Materials

1 shoe box per child, tempera paints, dish washing soap, large paintbrushes, 1 copy of the Bible verse Hebrews 13:16 per child, clear contact paper, glue, colored pencils

Preparation

1. Prepare the paint. Green, red, blue, and purple provide the best covering for the box. Add a small amount of dish washing soap to each color of paint to help it adhere to the box.
2. Paint each shoe box and let them dry.
3. Type the Bible verse and make one copy per child.

Directions

1. Give each child a copy of the Bible verse. Use the colored pencils to decorate it.
2. Cover each verse with contact paper.
3. Distribute the shoe boxes. Have the children glue the verse to the lid of the box.
4. Have the children use the paints to decorate their boxes. Let them dry for the remainder of the program.
5. The children may take the Sharing Boxes home and use them to collect things to share with other people (for example, candy, toys, books, money). Encourage children to share the contents of their boxes with family members and friends.

Do not neglect to do good and to share what you have, for such sacrifices are pleasing to God. —Hebrews 13:16

Linda

PROJECT: BASKETS TO SHARE

Materials

1 list of homebound or hospitalized church members, 1 basket per homebound or hospitalized person, ribbon, large pieces of colorful fabric, donated items (see examples below), large sheets of transparent wrapping paper, package wrapping, ribbons and bows, large sheets of white construction paper, scissors, crayons, colored markers, colorful stickers

Preparation

1. Ask church members to donate items for the baskets (for example, travel sized lotion, mouthwash etc., paperback books, puzzle books, pens and pencils, note cards, stamps, coloring books and crayons, small stuffed animals, toys, and so on) for the baskets. Publicize the gender and ages of intended recipients.

2. Arrange the items on a table. Group similar items together.

Directions

1. Give each child a piece of white construction paper.

2. Using the crayons, markers, and stickers, make get well or thinking-of-you cards. Use the list of homebound and hospitalized members as a guide for creating the cards.

3. Divide the children into groups. Give each group a basket, a piece of fabric, and ribbons. Place the fabric inside the basket so the edges hang over the sides. Attach ribbons to the basket handle.

4. Let each group select materials to put inside their basket. Remind the children to select items that would be appropriate for the person. Ask: Would Mr. Jamison like a crossword puzzle book or a coloring book? Which coloring book do you think your classmate Morgan would like?

5. Place a large piece of transparent wrapping paper on a table. Set the basket in the center of it. Gently gather up the edges and pull them up to the top. Secure it with ribbons and a big bow. Attach the card to the outside.

6. Arrange to have the baskets delivered by the pastor or visitation committee. Tell the recipients that these baskets are gifts from the children of your church.

BULLETIN BOARD: SHARING GOD'S LOVE

Materials

instant cameras, red and pink construction paper, attractive gift wrap paper, stapler or pushpins, letter stencils or dye cut machine, a copy of the Bible verse Hebrews 13:16 written in an attractive font

Preparation

1. Cut hearts out of the red and pink construction paper.

2. Attach the wrapping paper to the bulletin board as a background.

3. Make the title SHARING GOD'S LOVE from stencils or dye cut machine.

4. Attach the title, SHARING GOD'S LOVE, the Bible verse, and the hearts to the board.

Directions

1. Take instant photos of the kids making the cards and assembling the Baskets to Share. Attach these photos to the bulletin board with pushpins.

2. Take pictures of the basket recipients and attach them to the bulletin board. The kids will enjoy seeing pictures of the recipients of their sharing.

BULLETIN BOARD: SHARING GOD'S LOVE

SHARING GOD'S LOVE

PUZZLE: A MESSAGE TO REMEMBER

Follow the directions. Then print the message in the spaces to the right.

1. Cross out words that begin with the letter C.
2. Cross out words that end with the letter M.
3. Cross out words that have only one letter.
4. Cross out the word RUN each time you find it.
5. Cross out words that rhyme with SKY.

MY ROOM DO CAT COW RUN NOT NEGLECT I

BYE A TO RUN I DO HIGH GOOD AM RAM

COULD AND RYE A RUN LIE WHY SHY TO

AM SHARE RUN COLT WHAT BOOM YOU

FLY HAVE I FOR SUCH CANDY HAM A RUN

WHY SACRIFICES GUY ARE CAVE

PLEASING I TO SAM I A RUN GOD.

—Hebrews 13:16

From *Bible Verse Fun with Kids*. Copyright © 2004 by Cindy Dingwall. Reprinted by permission.

Appendix A

BIBLE VERSE GAMES

The three games in this appendix incorporate all twenty-five Bible verses in this book. Use the games after you have enjoyed all the lessons.

WALKING THE PATH

Materials

100 colored poster board squares (12 x 12 inches each), one copy of each Scripture reference (see Table of Contents), one copy of each Bible verse, fat felt black markers, laminating film and machine or clear contact paper, glue, dice (preferably large foam ones), an assortment of small inexpensive prizes

Preparation

1. Choose a large, easy-to-read computer font and print one copy of each Scripture reference and one copy of each Bible verse.

2. Glue a Bible verse to a colored poster board square. Glue the Scripture reference for that Bible verse to the back of that square.

3. Use the same easy-to-read font to create the following instructions:

- Jesus is born. Jump ahead three spaces to Bethlehem.
- You are lost in the desert. Go back two spaces.
- Jesus helped you cross the Jordan River. Go ahead four spaces.
- You were tempted to sin. Go back five spaces.

- You helped someone in need. Go ahead five spaces.
- You stopped to shop at the market place. Stay where you are for now.
- You stopped to have lunch with Jesus. Stay where you are for now.
- One of your sheep is missing. Go back three spaces to look for it.
- It's time to pray. Kneel down and stay put for now.
- You got lost looking for some misplaced coins. Go back one space.

(Think of 44 other instructions that will keep children in place or move them ahead or backward.)

4. Glue one set of instructions to each remaining card.

5. Laminate or cover each card with clear contact paper.

6. Place the cards on the floor in any pattern that accommodates the 100 cards, for example, a large square, a large circle, or set up as a winding path. Mix the instruction cards with the Bible verse and Scripture cards. See sample below.

Directions

1. Let four to six children play at one time. Have the first child roll the die, take that number of steps on the path, and then follow the instructions on the card he or she lands on. If the child lands on a Bible verse card, the child must read the verse aloud and identify the Scripture (the Bible book, chapter, and verse). The child receives a small prize if the answer is correct. If the child lands on the Scripture reference, he or she must recite the verse. Again, if the child is correct he or she wins a small prize. If the child lands on an instruction card, the child must do what the card indicates.

2. Let each child have a turn. See who can collect the most prizes, and who can finish the game first.

3. Consider rearranging the cards with each group of children that plays. Simply reverse the Scripture reference cards by turning them over. You can also rearrange the order of the cards for each group.

S = Scripture Reference
I = Instructions
V = Verse

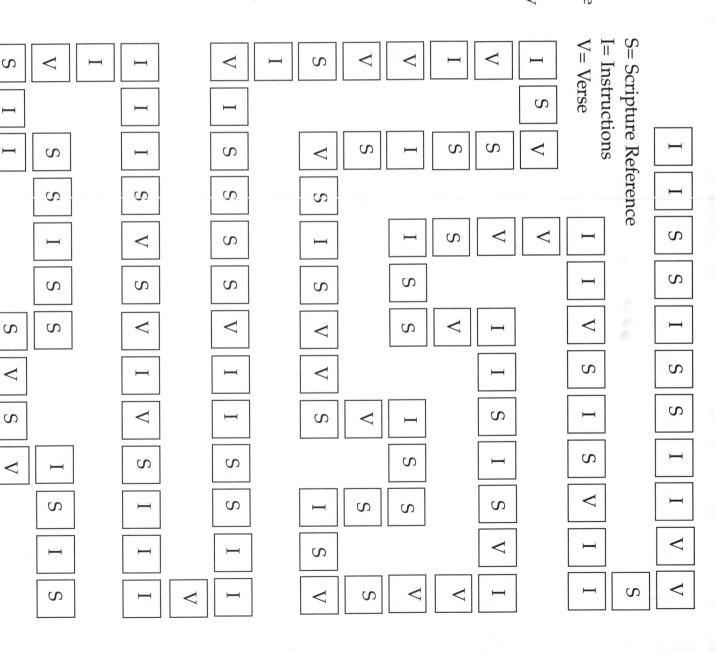

2. Put the pile of yellow cards in the center of the table.
3. Have each child draw a yellow card and read the Scripture reference printed on it. The child holding the green card that matches the Scripture reference says, "I MATCH!" That child wins both cards. If no one can match the verse to the Scripture reference, the card is placed at the bottom of the pile. Play until all cards are matched.
4. The child holding the most matched cards at the end of the game wins a large candy bar. Give the other children mini candy bars.

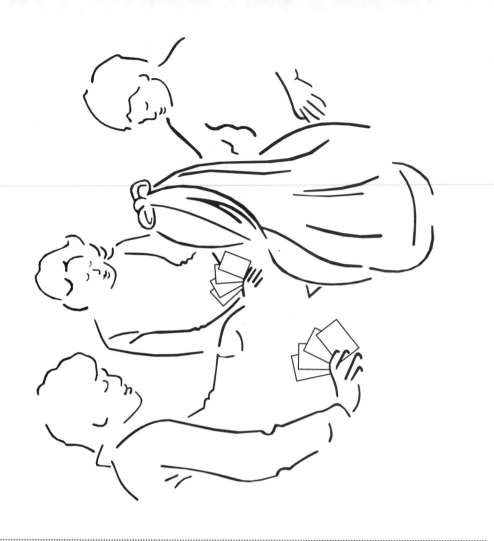

MATCH UPS GAME

Materials
26 green 4-by-6-inch index cards, 26 yellow 4-by-6-inch index cards, black marker, mini candy bars

Psalm 150:1

PRAISE THE LoRD!

Preparation
1. Print each Bible verse on a green card.
2. Print each Scripture reference (book, chapter, verse) on a yellow card.

Directions
1. The number of verses used in this game will depend on the number of children playing. For example, if you have twenty children playing, give ten children yellow cards and ten children green cards. Make sure the verse cards match the correct Scripture cards.
2. Tell the children to find their partners. The idea is for the children with Scripture cards to find the children with the correct verse cards and vice versa.
3. Give each pair of children who match up correctly a mini candy bar.

I MATCH

Materials
the green and yellow cards from the "Match Ups" game, a table and chairs, large candy bars, mini candy bars

Directions
1. Give each child several green cards. Divide the cards evenly among the children.

THE LONGEST BANNER EVER

Materials

1 large sheet of white construction paper per Bible verse, crayons, markers, stickers, tape, book tape, laminating film and machine or clear contact paper

Preparation

Use the markers to print a different Bible verse on each sheet of white paper.

Directions

1. Give each child a piece of white paper with a Scripture verse printed on it.
2. Tell the children to illustrate the verse printed on their paper. Laminate or cover each page with clear contact paper.
3. Place the finished pictures on a long table and tape the sides together to form a banner.
4. Turn the banner over. Tape the pages together along the backside. Place rolled up pieces of book tape along the backside of the banner.
5. Attach the banner to a long wall. Invite everyone to take a look at "the longest banner ever."

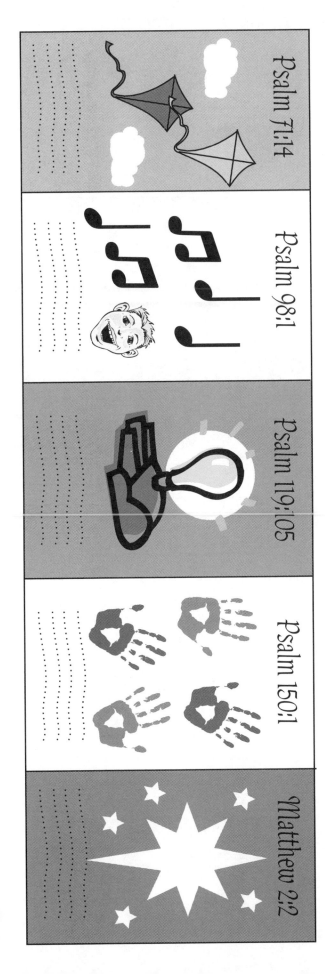

Psalm 71:14

Psalm 98:1

Psalm 119:105

Psalm 150:1

Matthew 2:2

BIBLE VERSE QUILT

Materials

twenty-six 12-inch square sheets of white card stock paper, sixty-four 12-inch squares of colored card stock paper, gift wrap paper, crayons, markers, tape, book tape, two or three large tables

Preparation

1. Use markers to print a Bible verse on each square of white card stock paper.

2. Place the tables together to make a large square table.

Directions

1. Give each child a piece of card stock with a Bible verse printed on it.

2. Let the children use crayons to illustrate the verse.

3. Lay the white verse cards on the table facing up. Mix in the other cards (solids, gift wrap, and so on) so that it looks like a big quilt. Tape the edges together.

4. Flip the quilt over, so it is face down. Tape the back edges together.

5. Attach rolled up book tape to the back of the quilt. Hang the quilt on a large wall in your building. Invite everyone to view "The Bible Verse Quilt."

V= Verse
GW= Giftwrap
S= Solid

V	S	GW	V	S
GW	V	S	GW	V
S	GW	V	S	GW
V	S	GW	V	S
GW	V	S	GW	V

BIBLE VERSE BOOKS

Materials

two 9-by-12-inch pieces of colored card stock per child, crayons, markers, stickers, hole punch, metal fasteners

Preparation

Print the words BIBLE VERSE FUN FOR KIDS on each sheet of card stock.

Directions

1. Give each child a sheet of card stock. Have the children print their names and use the crayons, markers, and stickers to decorate their sheets.

2. As you complete each lesson, let the children complete the puzzle that accompanies it.

3. Make a book of puzzles using the sheet they decorated as the cover. Let the children take their books home after completing the lessons in this book.

IDEA

After the children have finished their covers, add blank copies of each puzzle to the books. After you have finished sharing all of the lessons, give these to the kids. See how they do at working the puzzles, remembering the verses, and being able to tell about the lesson each verse has for us.

BIBLIOGRAPHY

A Child's Book of Prayers. Illustrated by Michael Hague. New York: Holt, Rinehart and Winston, 1985.

Aliki. Welcome, Little Baby. New York: Greenwillow Books, 1987.

All God's Children: A Book of Prayers. Selected by Lee Bennett Hopkins. San Diego: Harcourt Brace, 1998.

Anderson, Janet S. The Key into Winter. Morton Grove, Ill.: Albert Whitman, 1994.

Animal Patterns. Everett, Wash.: Warren Publishing House, 1990.

Applet, Kathi. Someone's Come to Our House. Grand Rapids: Eerdmans Books for Young Readers, 1999.

Bennett, William J. A Child's Book of Faith. New York: Doubleday Books for Young Readers, 2000.

Berenstain, Stan and Jan Berenstain. The Berenstain Bears and the Truth. New York: Random House, 1983.

The Big Book of Contemporary Christian Favorites. Milwaukee: Hal Leonard, 1995.

The Big Book of Hymns. Milwaukee: Hal Leonard, 1999.

Butler, Daphne. What Happens When Flowers Grow? Austin: Raintree Steck-Vaughn, 1995.

Carlson, Nancy. Hooray for Grandparent's Day. New York: Viking, 2000.

Carlstrom, Nancy White. Does God Know How to Tie Shoes? Grand Rapids: William B. Eerdmans, 1993.

Christian, Peggy. If You Find a Rock. San Diego: Harcourt, 2000.

Classic Treasury of Children's Prayers. Compiled by Susan Cuthbert. Minneapolis: Augsburg Fortress, 2000.

dePaola, Tomie. The Parables of Jesus. New York: Holiday House, 1987.

Edwards, Nancy. Glenna's Seeds. Washington, D.C.: Child & Family Press, 2001.

Ehlert, Lois. Planting a Rainbow. San Diego: Hartcourt Brace Jovanovich, 1988.

Everyday Patterns. Everett, Wash.: Warren Publishing House, 1990.

Favorite Hymns. Milwaukee: Hal Leonard, 1991.

Fowler, Allan. It Could Still Be a Rock. Chicago: Children's Press, 1993.

Ganeri, Anita. The Story of Christmas. New York: D. Kindersley, 1995.

Gibbons, Gail. From Seed to Plant. New York: Holiday House, 1991.

Giorgio, Gail. Footprints in the Sand. Carson City, N.Y.: Gold Leaf Press, 1995.

Graham, Bob. Spirit of Hope. Greenvale, N.Y.: Mondo, 1996.

Haidle, Helen. What Would Jesus Do? Grand Rapids: Zondervan, 1998.

Hall, Zoe. The Surprise Garden. New York: Blue Sky Press, 1998.

Handford, Martin. Where's Waldo? Cambridge, Mass.: Candlewick Press, 1997.

Harshman, Marc. Rocks in My Pockets. New York: Cobblehill Books/Dutton, 1991.

Helldorfer, Mary-Claire. Sailing to the Sea. New York: Viking, 1991.

Hoffman, Mary and Morris Jachu. Parables: Stories Jesus Told. New York: Phyllis Fogerman Books, 2000.

Holiday Patterns. Everett, Wash.: Warren Publishing House, 1990.

Kern, Noris. *I Love You with All My Heart.* San Francisco: Chronicle Books, 1998.

Keveren, Philip. *Timeless Praise.* Milwaukee, Wis.: Hal Leonard, 2001.

Kovacs, Deborah. *Moonlight on the River.* New York: Viking, 1993.

Lamstein, Sarah Marwil. *I Like Your Buttons!* Morton Grove, Ill.: A. Whitman, 1999.

Le Tord, Bijou. *God's Little Seeds: A Book of Parables.* Grand Rapids: William B. Eerdmans Books for Young Readers, 1998.

Littlesugar, Amy. *Tree of Hope.* New York: Philomel, 1999.

McCourt, Lisa. *The Best Night Out with Dad.* Dearfield Beach, Fla.: Health Communications, 1997.

Macdonald, Maryann. *Rosie and the Poor Rabbits.* New York: Atheneum, 1991.

McGovern, Ann. *The Lady in the Box.* New York: Turtle Books, 1997.

Mason, Antony. *If You Were There: Biblical Times.* New York: Simon & Schuster Books for Young Readers, 1996.

Mayper, Monica. *Come and See: A Christmas Story.* New York: HarperCollins, 1999.

Melmed, Laura. *The First Song Ever Sung.* New York: Lothrop, Lee & Shepherd Books, 1993.

Oberman, Sheldon. *The Always Prayer Shawl.* Honesdale, Pa.: Caroline House, 1994.

Oppenheim, Shulamith Levy. *Fireflies for Nathan.* New York: Tambourine Books, 1994.

Parnell, Peter. *The Rock.* New York: Macmillan, 1991.

Peter, Lisa Westburg. *Meg and Dad Discover Treasure in the Air.* New York: H. Holt, 1995.

Peterson, Jeanne Whitehouse. *My Mama Sings.* New York: HarperCollins, 1994.

Price, Lynn Hope. *These Hands.* New York: Hyperion Books for Children, 1999.

Rand, Gloria. *Aloha, Salty!* New York: H. Holt, 1996.

———. *Salty Sails North.* New York: H. Holt, 1990.

Raposo, Joe. *The Sesame Street Songbook.* New York: Simon and Schuster, 1971.

Schwartz, Stephen. *Vocal Selections from Godspell.* Winona, Minn.: H. Leonard, 1971.

Sharmat, Marjorie Weinman. *The Big Fat Enormous Lie.* New York: Dutton, 1986.

Stevens, Janet. *The Tortoise and the Hare.* New York: Holiday House, 1991.

Stevenson, Mary. *The Illustrated Footprints in the Sand.* New York: William Morris, 1998.

They Followed a Bright Star. Based on a poem by Joan Alavedra. New York: Putnam, 1994.

Thomas, Jean Monrad. *A Child's Book of Hope.* New York: Random House, 1999.

Thompson, Lauren. *Love One Another: The Last Days of Jesus.* New York: Scholastic Press, 2000.

Warren, Jean. *Nature Patterns.* Everett, Wash.: Warren Publishing House, 1990.

Wildsmith, Brian. *The Easter Story.* New York: A. A. Knopf, 1994.

———. *The Hare and the Tortoise.* London: Oxford University Press, 1995.

Williamson, Marianne. *Emma and Mommy Talk to God.* New York: HarperCollins, 1996.

Winthrop, Elizabeth. *He Is Risen.* New York: Holiday House, 1985.

Zolotow, Charlotte. *Say It!* New York: Greenwillow Books, 1980.

RESOURCE LIST

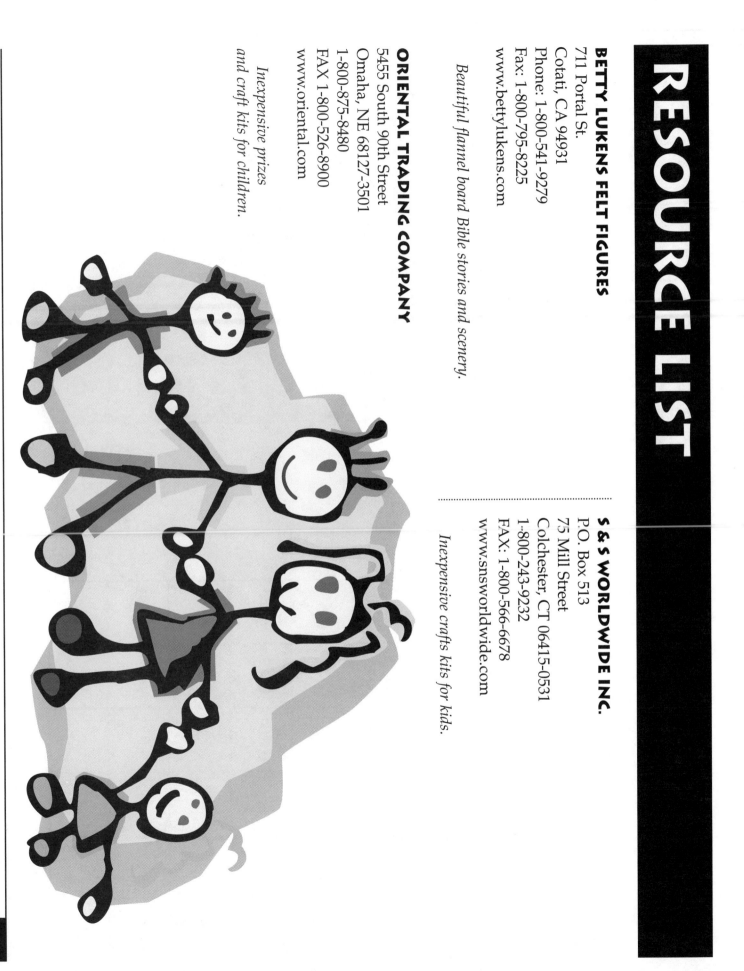

BETTY LUKENS FELT FIGURES

711 Portal St.
Cotati, CA 94931
Phone: 1-800-541-9279
Fax: 1-800-795-8225
www.bettylukens.com

Beautiful flannel board Bible stories and scenery.

ORIENTAL TRADING COMPANY

5455 South 90th Street
Omaha, NE 68127-3501
1-800-875-8480
FAX 1-800-526-8900
www.oriental.com

*Inexpensive prizes
and craft kits for children.*

S & S WORLDWIDE INC.

P.O. Box 513
75 Mill Street
Colchester, CT 06415-0531
1-800-243-9232
FAX: 1-800-566-6678
www.snsworldwide.com

Inexpensive crafts kits for kids.

PUZZLE SOLUTIONS

CHAPTER 1
PUZZLE: LET'S TAKE A WALK
PAGE 13

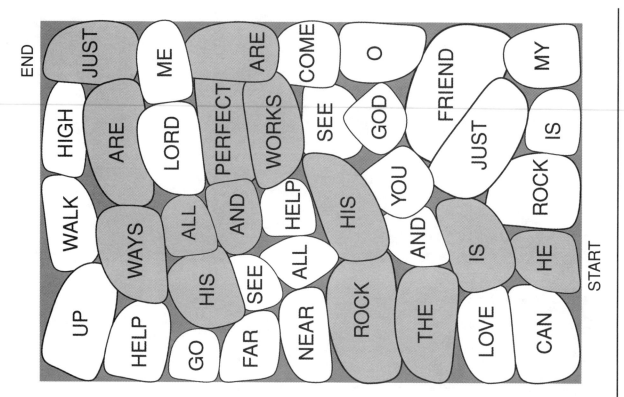

**CHAPTER 2
PUZZLE:
ROCKIN'
WITH GOD
PAGE 17**

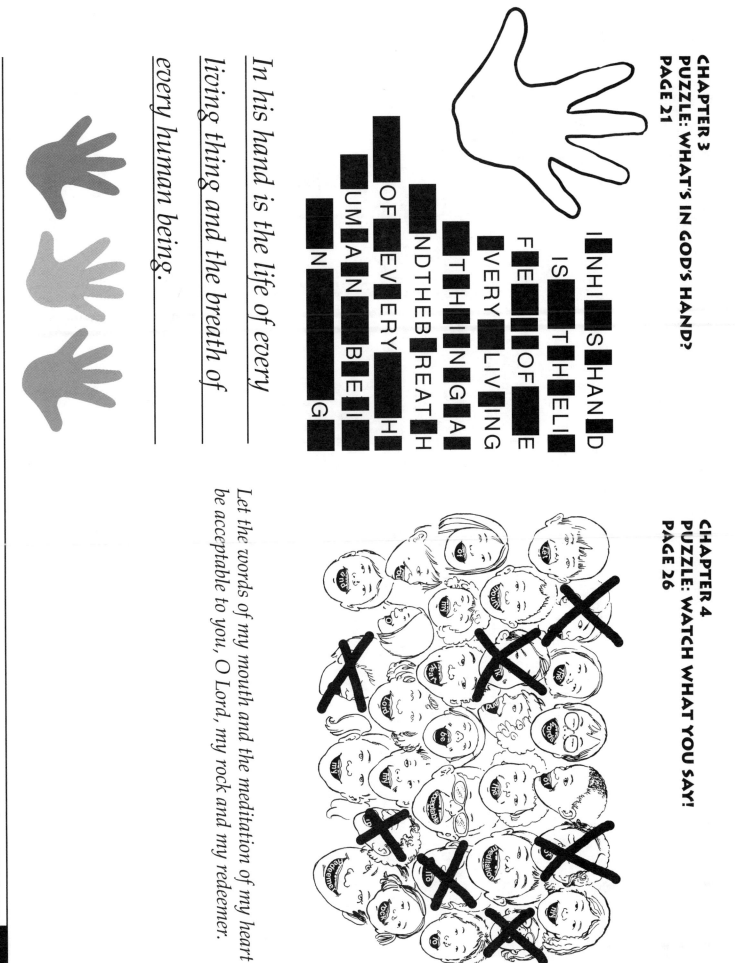

I N HI S HAN D
IS T H ELI
F E E OF E
VERY LIVING
THING A
NDTHEB REAT H
OF EVERY H
UM A N B E I
N G

In his hand is the life of every

living thing and the breath of

every human being.

Let the words of my mouth and the meditation of my heart

be acceptable to you, O Lord, my rock and my redeemer.

1=A 4=D 7=G 10=J 13=M 16=P 19=S 22=V 25=Y

2=B 5=E 8=H 11=K 14=N 17=Q 20=T 23=W 26=Z

3=C 6=F 9=I 12=L 15=O 18=R 21=U 24=X

H E A R   M Y   P R A Y E R,   O   G O D:
8 5 1 18   13 25   16 18 1 25 5 18   15   7 15 4

G I V E   E A R   T O   T H E   W O R D S
7 9 22 5   5 1 18   20 15   20 8 5   23 15 18 4 19

O F   M Y   M O U T H.
15 6   13 25   13 15 21 20 8

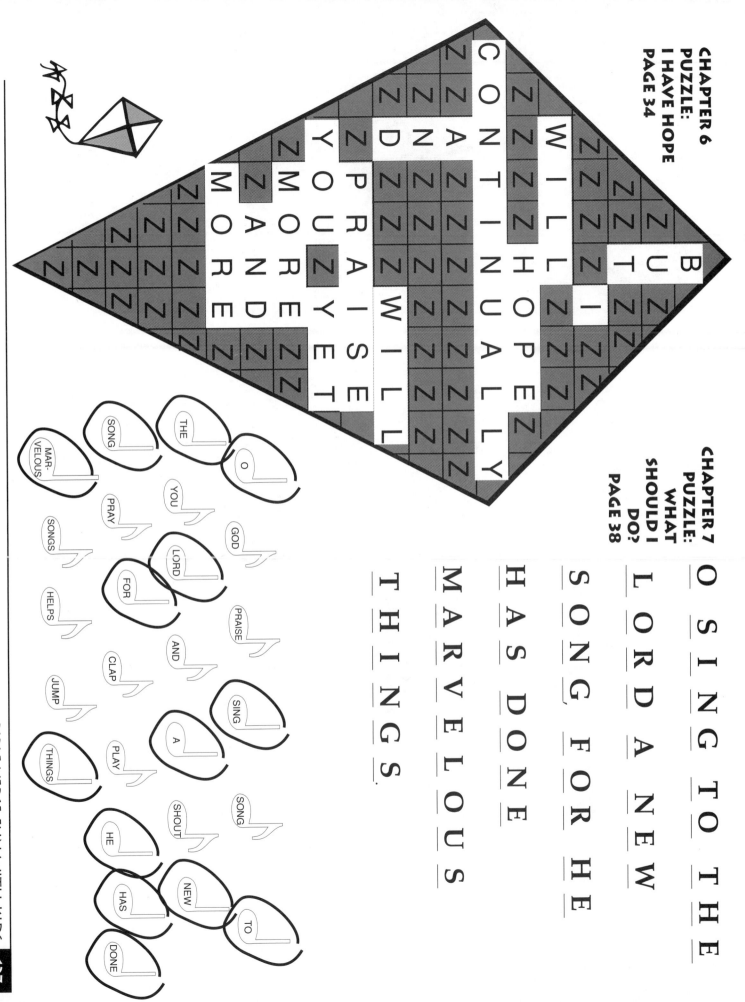

CHAPTER 6
PUZZLE:
I HAVE HOPE
PAGE 34

CHAPTER 7
PUZZLE:
WHAT
SHOULD I
DO?
PAGE 38

O S I N G T O T H E

L O R D A N E W

S O N G F O R H E

H A S D O N E

M A R V E L O U S

T H I N G S .

SONG THE O YOU GOD PRAISE AND CLAP JUMP SING A PLAY SONG SHOUT HE NEW TO DONE HAS LORD FOR HELPS SONGS PRAY MAR-VELOUS THINGS

I HAVE CHOSEN THE

WAY OF TRUTH; I

HAVE SET MY HEART

ON YOUR LAWS.

TRUE statements:

1, 4, 5, 6, 8, 9, 10, 12, 13, 15, 16,

17, 19, 21, 24

CHAPTER 9 PUZZLE: GOD'S LIGHT GUIDES ME PAGE 47

1. Let the light of Y O U R face shine upon us,
   O LORD! (Psalm 4:6)

2. You are my hiding place and my shield; I hope in your
   W O R D . (Psalm 119:114)

3. The LORD I S God, and he has given us light. (Psalm 118:27)

4. Your word is A lamp to my feet and a light to my path. (Psalm 119:105)

5. Indeed, you are my L A M P , O LORD, the LORD lightens my darkness. (2 Samuel 22:29)

6. Be very careful, therefore, T O love the LORD your God. (Joshua 23:11)

7. The LORD is M Y light and my salvation; whom shall I fear? (Psalm 27:1)

8. My steps have held fast to your paths; my F E E T have not slipped. (Psalm 17:5)

9. Your word is a lamp to my feet A N D a A light to my path. (Psalm 119:105)

10. Arise, shine; for your L I G H T has come, and the glory of the LORD has risen upon you.
    (Isaiah 60:1)

11. I hurry and do not delay T O keep your commandments. (Psalm 119:60)

12. The LORD is M Y shepherd, I shall not want.
    (Psalm 23:1)

13. Lead me in the P A T H of your commandments; for I delight in it. (Psalm 119:35)

YOUR WORD IS A LAMP TO MY FEET

AND A LIGHT TO MY PATH. —*Psalm 119:105*

```
G  O  T  O  C  H  U  R  C  H
I [P  R  A  I  S  E] *  O  *  H
V  J  C  L  A  P  A  I  M  T  E
E  U  P  R  A  Y  *  *  F  H
S  M  L  E  A  R  N  W  O  E
I  P  L  A  Y  H  R  A  R  S
N  *  *  D  *  O  U  L  T
*  *  *  P  N  K  *  F  A
G  A  S  K  *  *  N  W  O
F  R  I  E  N  D  L  Y  R  A
[L  O  R  D] H  E  L  P  *  E
```

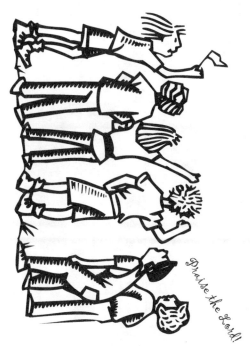

Praise the Lord!

Hidden words: WE SAW HIS STAR IN THE EAST AND HAVE COME TO WORSHIP HIM

- W O R S H I P
- T O
- H A V E
- E A S T
- H I S
- W E
- S A W
- H I M
- C O M E
- A N D
- T H E
- I N
- S T A R

CHAPTER 12

PUZZLE: WHAT CAN WE DO?
PAGE 60

Ask, and it will be given you; search, and you will find; knock, and the door will be opened. — Matthew 7:7

GOD
YOU
LOVE
HOPE
FAITH
LORD
LEARN
WOW
JESUS
CREATOR
JOY
LOOK
HELPER
REDEEMER
FORGIVES
KINGDOM
HAPPY
SAVIOR
CARES
KING
FRIEND
PRAY

I WILL GIVE YOU THE KEYS OF THE KINGDOM OF HEAVEN.

```
X C X J X J C X C J X
X C C X J C C C X J J
C O D C C J X J J T C
J X O J X J J C T J X
C C X C C C C J H C J
J X J J J H C X C M X
G C J X C X C C X C X
N C J C X X O C X J C
J X X X E J X X C J J
C J K J X E C C X J X
C C X C J C C X J C X
X C O X J C J C J C X
X J X M C X C C J C C
```

For truly I tell you, if you have faith the size of a mustard seed, you will say to this mountain, "Move from here to there," and it will move; and nothing will be impossible for you.
—Matthew 17:20

● = BLACK   ■ = BLUE

	TELL					
		MUSTARD	SAY		HERE	WILL
TELL	YOU	OF	SEED	MOVE	THERE	AND	IMPOSSIBLE
FOR	HAVE	SIZE	TO		TO	AND	MOVE	WILL
TRULY	YOU	FAITH		YOU	THIS		IT	
I	IF		A	MOUNTAIN			
THE	YOU	WILL		FROM			BE	NOTHING	YOU

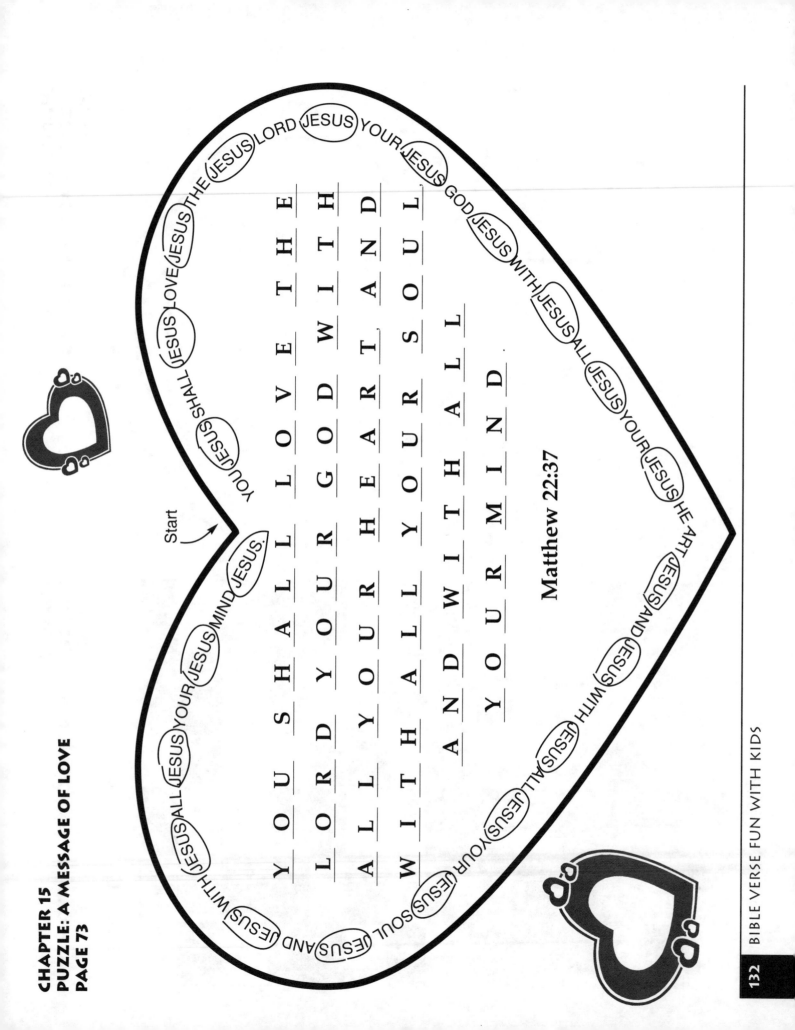

Start

YOU SHALL LOVE THE LORD YOUR GOD WITH ALL YOUR HEART AND WITH ALL YOUR SOUL AND WITH ALL YOUR MIND.

Matthew 22:37

TSIRHC C H R I S T
ERODA A D O R E
EM M E
DEKLAW W A L K E D
TIRIPS S P I R I T
REHCAET T E A C H E R
EPOH H O P E
UOY Y O U
YEBO O B E Y
MELASUREJ J E R U S A L E M
YBAB B A B Y
NRAEL L E A R N
RENNIW W I N N E R
RETSAE E A S T E R
YRAM M A R Y
SUSEJ J E S U S
SAMTSIRHC C H R I S T M A S
ROIVAS S A V I O R
HTURT T R U T H
DREHPEHS S H E P H E R D
REGNAM M A N G E R
TSAEF F E A S T
NEVAEH H E A V E N
DOG G O D
YEKNOD D O N K E Y

REHTAF F A T H E R
RATS S T A R
PLEH H E L P
MIEHELHTEB B E T H L E H E M
SELCARIM M I R A C L E S
DOOG G O O D
EGARUOC C O U R A G E

I AM WITH YOU
ALWAYS,
TO THE END OF
THE AGE." (Matthew 28:20)

YOU SHALL
LOVE YOUR
NEIGHBOR AS
YOURSELF

NEIGHBOR AS YOU SHALL ... LOVE YOUR NEIGHBOR ... YOURSELF

For God so loved the world that he gave his only Son so that everyone who believes in him may not perish but may have eternal life.

4 God _so_ loved the

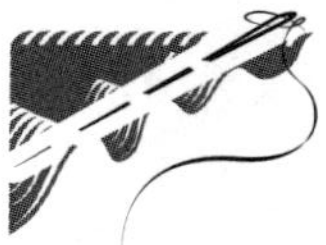

For 🌍 _world_ that he gave his only

Son _so_ that every1 everyone

that every1 everyone

who believes in him

not _ish_ but may _perish_

may

have eternal life. –John 3:16

MAY
S M T W T F S
1 2 3 4 5 6 7
8 9 10 11 12 13 14
15 16 17 18 19 20 21
22 23 24 25 26 27
29 30 31

You will have joy and

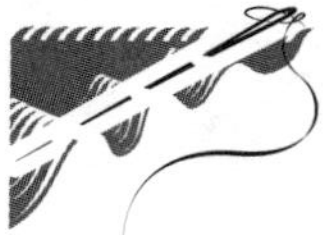

gladness, and many

will rejoice at his

birth.

A N D

JOY

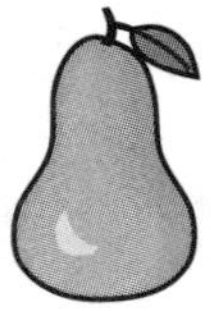

WILL

BIRTH

HAVE

M A N Y

HIS

WILL

AND

AT

YOU

GLADNESS

REJOICE

■ PINK

■ YELLOW

The point is this:
the one who sows
sparingly will also
reap sparingly,
and the one who
sows bountifully
will also reap
bountifully.
2 Corinthians 9:6

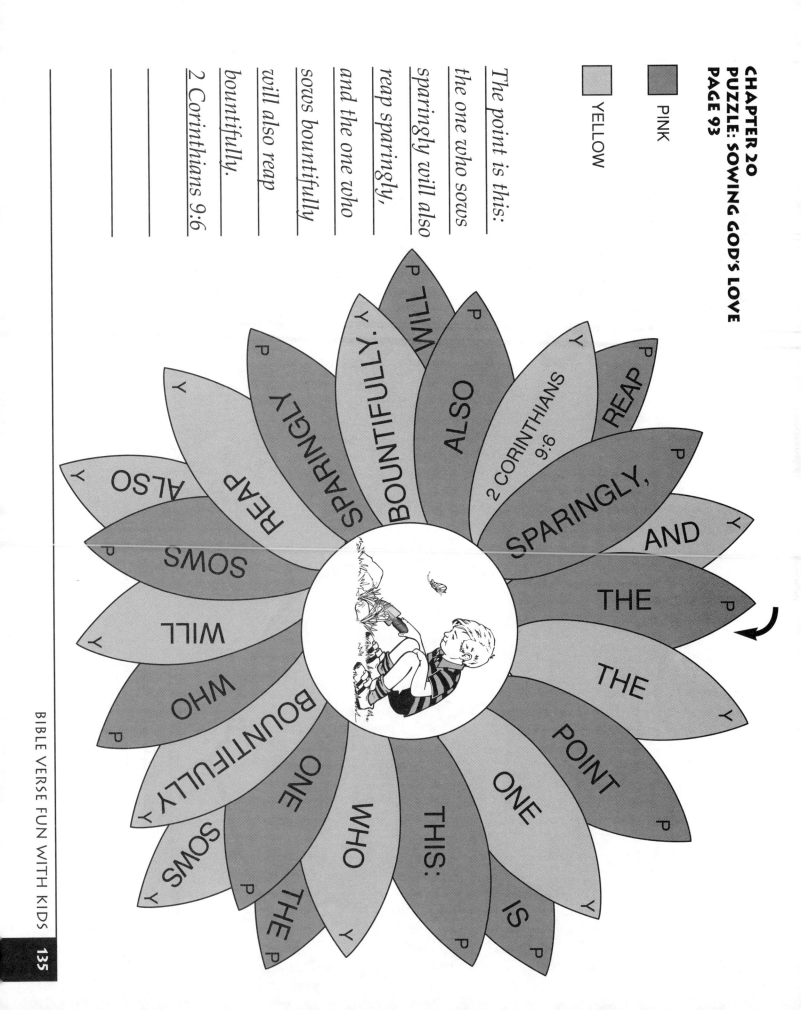

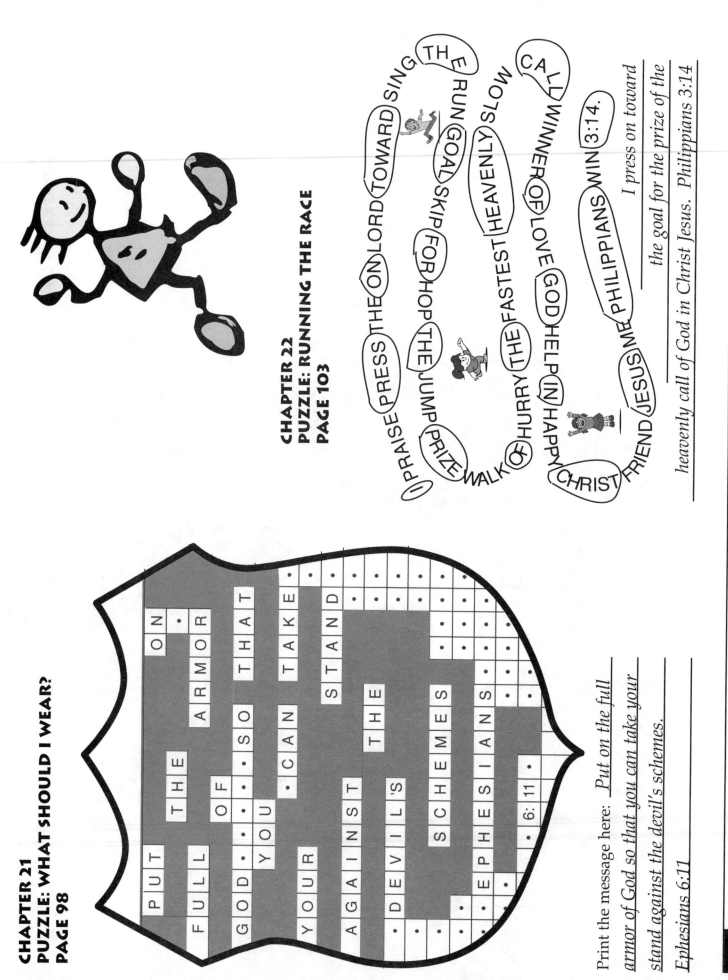

Print the message here: _Put on the full_
armor of God so that you can take your
stand against the devil's schemes.
Ephesians 6:11

I press on toward _____
the goal for the prize of the _____
heavenly call of God in Christ Jesus. Philippians 3:14

~~FROG~~ AS ~~ZEBRA TOES~~ GOD'S ~~HEAD~~ CHOSEN ONES ~~SHARK~~ HOLY ~~HANDS NOSE~~ AND ~~DARK EYES~~ BELOVED ~~MARK~~

~~CLOTHING~~ CLOTHE ~~ZIP~~ ~~THANKSGIVING~~ YOURSELVES ~~THE~~ WITH ~~ZIPPERS RED~~ COMPASSION ~~GREEN~~ KINDNESS

~~BLUE FEET~~ HUMILITY ~~TWO PURPLE~~ MEEKNESS ~~ZONE FOG~~ AND ~~ORANGE~~ PATIENCE ~~EASTER FOG.~~

Print the verse in the spaces below.

A S G O D ' S C H O S E N O N E S ,

H O L Y A N D B E L O V E D ,

C L O T H E Y O U R S E L V E S

W I T H C O M P A S S I O N ,

K I N D N E S S , H U M I L I T Y ,

M E E K N E S S , A N D

P A T I E N C E .

Colossians 3:12

CHAPTER 24
PUZZLE: WHAT DO WE HAVE?
PAGE 111

3, 4	WE	2	FOR
7	HAVE	4, 5	THE
2, 3	THIS	6	SOUL
5	HOPE	1	FIRM
6, 7	AS	5, 6	AND
1, 2	AN	3	SECURE
4	ANCHOR		

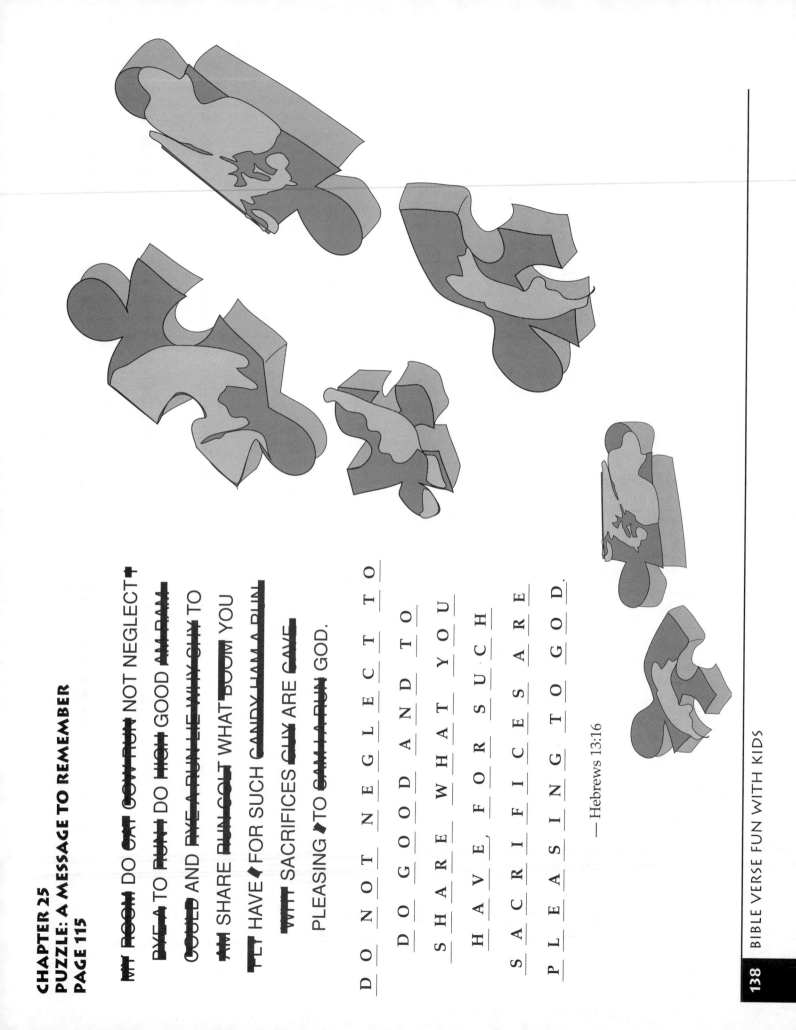

MY ROOM DO EAT COMFORT NOT NEGLECT ✝

BREAD TO PUSH DO HIGH GOOD AND RAIN

COOKS AND RYE ARE LIKELY SUN TO

AM SHARE RUN OUT WHAT BOOM YOU

FLY HAVE ✦ FOR SUCH CANDY I AM A RUN

WIT SACRIFICES GUY ARE CAVE

PLEASING ▶ TO SAND A RUN GOD.

D O N O T N E G L E C T T O

D O G O O D A N D T O

S H A R E W H A T Y O U

H A V E , F O R S U C H

S A C R I F I C E S A R E

P L E A S I N G T O G O D .

— Hebrews 13:16

SCRIPTURE INDEX

OLD TESTAMENT

NEW TESTAMENT

TOPIC INDEX

Subjects are in CAPITAL LETTERS.